PHAEDRUS

PLATO

PHAEDRUS

TRANSLATED BY WALTER HAMILTON

PENGUIN BOOKS

PENGUIN BOOKS

Published by the Penguin Group

Penguin Books USA Inc., 375 Hudson Street,
New York, New York 10014, U.S.A.
Penguin Books Ltd, 27 Wrights Lane,
London W8 5TZ, England
Penguin Books Australia Ltd, Ringwood,
Victoria, Australia
Penguin Books Canada Ltd, 10 Alcorn Avenue,
Toronto, Ontario, Canada M4V 3B2
Penguin Books (N.Z.) Ltd, 182–190 Wairau Road,
Auckland 10, New Zealand

Penguin Books Ltd, Registered Offices:
Harmondsworth, Middlesex, England

Published in Penguin Books 1995

This extract is from Walter Hamilton's translation of *Phaedrus and Letters VII and VIII* by Plato, published by Penguin Books.

ISBN 0 14 60.0179 6

Printed in the United States of America

Phaedrus

Prelude

SOCRATES: Where have you come from, my dear Phaedrus, and where are you going?

PHAEDRUS: I have been with Lysias, the son of Cephalus, Socrates, and I am going for a walk outside the walls after a long session with him that has lasted since early morning. Our common friend, Acumenus, says that a country walk is more refreshing than a stroll in the city squares; that is why I am going in this direction.

SOCRATES: Acumenus is quite right, my friend. So Lysias was in the city, was he?

PHAEDRUS: Yes, he was visiting Epicrates, in the house you see there near the temple of Olympian Zeus, the house that used to belong to Morychus.

SOCRATES: What were you doing there? Lysias was entertaining you with his eloquence, I suppose?

PHAEDRUS: You shall hear, if you can spare the time to go with me.

SOCRATES: Spare the time! Don't you realize that to me an account of what passed between you and Lysias is, to use Pindar's phrase, 'a matter which takes precedence even over business'?

PHAEDRUS: Come along then.

SOCRATES: Your story, please.

PHAEDRUS: Well, Socrates, what I have to tell is very much in your line, for the subject on which we were engaged was love – after a fashion. Lysias has written a speech designed to win the favour of a handsome boy for someone who is not in love with him. That is the clever thing about it; he makes out that an admirer who is not in love is to be preferred to one who is.

SOCRATES: Noble fellow! I only wish he would prove that a poor lover is preferable to a rich, and an old lover to a young, and deal in the same way with all the other disadvantages under which I, like most of us, labour. Then his speeches would be delightful indeed and a blessing to the public. Really, I have conceived such a passionate desire to hear your account that even if you prolong your walk as far as the walls of Megara and then, in the manner of Herodicus, turn straight back, I won't be left behind.

PHAEDRUS: Come, come, my good Socrates. Do you suppose that an amateur like me can adequately reproduce what it took Lysias, the best writer living, so much time and study to compose? Of course not. Yet I'd rather be able to do that than come into a fortune.

SOCRATES: My dear Phaedrus, I know my Phaedrus as well as I know my own name. And that being so I'm convinced that he wasn't content with a single hearing of Lysias' speech but made him repeat it a number of times, and that Lysias willingly complied. But even that didn't satisfy Phaedrus, and in the end he took the manuscript and went over his favourite passages by himself. Finally, exhausted by sitting at this occupation since early morning, he went out for a walk with the whole speech, I could swear, firmly in his head, unless it was excessively long. His motive in going outside the walls was to be able to declaim it aloud. Imagine his delight when he met a man whose passion for such speeches amounts to a disease; now he would have someone to share his enthusiasm, so he asked him to go along with him. But when the speech-lover asked him to repeat the speech he grew coy and affected reluctance, though in fact he meant to force it on his companion in the end, whether he wanted it or not. So now, Phaedrus, beg him to do without further delay what he is eventually going to do in any case.

PHAEDRUS: Well, the only course for me is to repeat the speech as best I can, since you clearly won't let me go till I have given you some sort of satisfaction.

SOCRATES: You need be in no doubt about that.

PHAEDRUS: Well, this is what I will do. I didn't learn the speech by heart, Socrates, I assure you, but I will summarize point by point from the beginning the argument of almost all that Lysias said about the superiority of the man not in love to the man in love.

SOCRATES: Yes, but before you begin on that, dear heart, just let me see what it is you are holding in your left hand under your cloak; I strongly suspect it is the actual speech. If I am right you can make up your mind to this, that, much as I love you, I have no intention of letting you use me to rehearse on when I might have Lysias himself. Come on, show me.

PHAEDRUS: Enough of that. You've dashed my hope of using you to practise on, Socrates. Where would you like us to sit down and read?

SOCRATES: Let us turn aside here along the Ilissus. Then we can sit down in peace wherever we feel inclined.

PHAEDRUS: It's lucky I came out without shoes. You, of course, never wear them. Our easiest way is to get our feet wet and walk in the stream. Pleasant enough too, especially at this hour and time of year.

SOCRATES: Go ahead, and look out for a place for us to sit.

PHAEDRUS: Do you see that very tall plane tree?

SOCRATES: What about it?

PHAEDRUS: There is shade there and a gentle breeze, and grass to sit on, or lie, if we prefer.

SOCRATES: Lead on then.

PHAEDRUS: Tell me, Socrates, isn't there a story that Boreas abducted Oreithyia from somewhere here on the banks of the Ilissus?

SOCRATES: So they say.

PHAEDRUS: Was it here, do you think? The water is delightfully fresh and clear, just the place for girls to play.

SOCRATES: No, it was some quarter of a mile downstream, where one crosses to the temple of Agra; an altar to Boreas marks the spot, I believe.

PHAEDRUS: I haven't noticed it. But seriously, Socrates, do you believe this legend?

SOCRATES: The pundits reject it, so if I rejected it too I should be in good company. In that case I should rationalize the legend by explaining that the north wind blew Oreithyia down the neighbouring rocks when she was playing with Pharmaceia, and that her dying in this way was the origin of the legend that she was abducted by Boreas. (Or else she fell from the Areopagus, for according to one version the abduction took place from the Areopagus, not from here.) But though I find such explanations very attractive, Phaedrus, they are too ingenious and laboured, it seems to me, and I don't altogether envy the man who devotes himself to this sort of work, if only because, when he has finished with Oreithyia, he must go on to put the Hippocentaurs into proper shape and after them the Chimaera. In fact he finds himself overwhelmed by a host of Gorgons and Pegasuses and other such

4

monsters, whose numbers create no less a problem than their grotesqueness, and a sceptic who proposes to force each one of them into a plausible shape with the aid of a sort of rough ingenuity will need a great deal of leisure. Now I have no time for such work, and the reason is, my friend, that I've not yet succeeded in obeying the Delphic injunction to 'know myself', and it seems to me absurd to consider problems about other beings while I am still in ignorance about my own nature. So I let these things alone and acquiesce in the popular attitude towards them; as I've already said I make myself rather than them the object of my investigations, and I try to discover whether I am a more complicated and puffed-up sort of animal than Typho or whether I am a gentler and simpler creature, endowed by heaven with a nature altogether less typhonic. But while we are talking, my friend, haven't we reached the tree that you were making for?

PHAEDRUS: This is the very place.

SOCRATES: It is indeed a lovely spot for a rest. This plane is very tall and spreading, and the agnus-castus splendidly high and shady, in full bloom too, filling the neighbourhood with the finest possible fragrance. And the spring which runs under the plane; how beautifully cool its water is to the feet. The figures and other offerings show that the place is sacred to Achelous and some of the nymphs. See too how wonderfully delicate and sweet the air is, throbbing in response to the shrill chorus of the cicadas – the very voice of summer. But the most exquisite thing of all is the way the grass slopes gently upward to provide perfect comfort for the head as one lies at length. Really, my dear Phaedrus, a visitor could not possibly have found a better guide than you.

PHAEDRUS: What a very strange person you are, Socrates. So

far from being like a native, you resemble, in your own phrase, a visitor being shown the sights by a guide. This comes of your never going abroad beyond the frontiers of Attica or even, as far as I can see, outside the actual walls of the city.

SOCRATES: Forgive me, my dear friend. I am, you see, a lover of learning. Now the people in the city have something to teach me, but the fields and trees won't teach me anything. All the same you have found a way to charm me into making an expedition. Men lead hungry animals by waving a branch or some vegetable before their noses, and it looks as if you will lead me all over Attica and anywhere else you please in the same way by waving the leaves of a speech in front of me. For the moment, however, having got as far as this, I mean to lie down; so choose whatever position you think will be most comfortable for the purpose and read to me.

THE SPEECH OF LYSIAS

PHAEDRUS: Listen then.

'You know my situation, and you have heard how I think that it will be to our advantage for this to happen. I beg you not to reject my suit because I am not in love with you. Lovers repent the kindnesses they have shown when their passion abates, but to men not in love there never comes a time for such regret. They behave as generously as their means allow, not under constraint but with their eyes open, after deliberate calculation of their own interests. Again, lovers bring into account not only the kindnesses they have shown but also the losses they have incurred in their own affairs on account of their passion, and when they add to this the trouble they have undergone they consider that the debt they owe to their favourites has been discharged long ago. Those who are not in love, on the other hand, cannot use as a pretext for coolness the excuse that love has made them neglect their own interests, or put into the reckoning the hardships they have endured, or hold the loved one responsible for their having quarrelled with their families; and since they are relieved from all these disadvantages nothing remains for them but to do cheerfully whatever they think will give their partners pleasure. Again, if lovers deserve to be made much of because they declare that whoever they are in love with has a supreme claim on their friendship, and because they are prepared to say and do what will incur the hostility of others in order to please their beloved, then, if their professions are genuine, the conclusion plainly follows that they will value any new love in future more than the old, and even be ready to inflict an injury on the old love if the new love requires it. And how can it be sensible in a matter of such importance to trust oneself to a man suffering from a disorder of a kind that no experienced person would even attempt to cure? Lovers themselves admit that they are mad, not sane, and that they know that they are not in their right mind but cannot help themselves. How then can one expect that designs formed in such a condition will meet with their approval when they come to their senses? Besides, if you choose the best from among your lovers, you will have few to choose from, whereas, if you look for the man who suits you best in the world at large, you will have a wide field of choice, and so a much better chance of finding in it the man who is worthy of your friendship.

'Now, if you are afraid that public opinion will condemn you when men hear of your love affairs, reflect that the lover, believing that others will envy his good fortune as much as he values it himself, is likely in a state of elation and gratified pride to publish generally the fact that his efforts have not gone unrewarded, whereas the man not in love, having better control of himself, will probably subordinate reputation to what is in fact the best course. Again, numbers of people will inevitably see or hear of the lover persistently dogging the footsteps of his beloved, so that whenever they are observed talking to one another it will be supposed that they are together because they have just gratified or are about to gratify their passion; those not in love incur no blame at all for keeping company, since people realize that one man may have occasion to talk to another because he is his friend or because the conversation gives him pleasure for some other reason. Then again, you may be alarmed by the reflection that friendships are easily broken, and that if that happens the greater part of the harm will fall on you, who have sacrificed your dearest possession, whereas a quarrel in other circumstances is a misfortune shared by both parties equally. In that case you have all the more reason to be afraid of those who are in love with you; they can be hurt in such a variety of ways and are apt to interpret anything as a personal slight. That is why they do not like their favourites to consort with anyone else; they may be outbidden by the rich or found inferior in intelligence to the educated, and similarly they are on their guard against the possessor of any other advantage. If they succeed in getting you to break with such people, you are left without a friend in the world; if you consult your own interests, and show more sense than your lovers, you will quarrel with *them*. Those not in love, on the other hand, who owe their success in their suit to their own good qualities, so far from being jealous of your associates, will hate those who shun your society; they will feel slighted themselves by such behaviour and positively obliged by those who cultivate you. So such an affair as I suggest is much more likely to win you friends than enemies.

'Besides, with most of your lovers physical attraction will have preceded any knowledge of your character or acquaintance with your circumstances; it must therefore be uncertain whether they will want to remain your friends when their passion has cooled. But those not in love, who were friends before they formed a liaison, are in no danger of finding their friendship diminished as a result of the satisfaction they have enjoyed; on the contrary, the recollection of it will be a pledge of further satisfaction to come. Moreover, you have a better chance of improving yourself by yielding to me than by yielding to a lover. Lovers approve words and actions that are far from excellent, partly because they are afraid of getting themselves disliked and partly because their passion impairs their judgement. One of love's feats is this: it makes lovers, when they are out of luck, treat as grievances things which cause no pain to ordinary men; when they are fortunate it compels them to bestow praise on things which do not deserve even the name of pleasant. So those who are in love are far more to be pitied than admired by the objects of their passion. But if you yield to *my* suit you will find that I, being my own master and not under the dominion of love, shall in all our dealings have an eye more to future advantage than to present pleasure. I shall not allow trifling causes to engender violent hostility; on the contrary, I shall be slow to exhibit a small degree of anger even on serious provocation; offence given involuntarily I shall overlook, and intentional slights I shall endeavour to avert; this is the way to lay the foundation of lasting affection. If you are possessed by the notion that firm friendship is impossible unless one is in love, let me remind you that in that case we should have little regard for our sons, or our fathers and mothers, nor should we have made loyal friends whose friendship is based not on passion but on associations of quite a different kind.

'Again, if you hold that we should show favour to those who press their suit most strongly, we must extend this principle further and show kindness not to the most deserving but to the most necessitous, whose gratitude will be proportionate to the severity of the hardships from which we relieve them. Not only so, but when we give a private party our guests should be not our friends but beggars in need of a good meal; they are the people who will love us for it and attach themselves to us and come about our doors; they will be the best pleased and the most grateful, and will call down countless blessings on the head of their host. Nevertheless, the truth may be that it is not the most insistent that you should favour, but those best able to make a return; not lovers merely, but those who show themselves worthy of what they ask; not those who will simply enjoy your youthful charms, but those who will share their possessions with you when you are older; not those who will boast of their success to others, but those whom modesty will keep completely silent; not those who are keen on you just for the moment, but those who will remain your firm friends for life; not those who will look for an excuse to break with you when their passion wanes, but those who will show themselves good men and true when your good looks have vanished. Remember what I have said, and bear in mind too that lovers are liable to be reproached by their friends for the sorry state they are in, whereas those who are not in love are never blamed by any of their relatives on the ground that they are neglecting their true interests.

'Perhaps you may ask whether I advise you to yield indiscriminately to anyone who is not in love. No more, I answer, than the lover would urge you to show such a disposition to all who *are* in love; such behaviour would lessen your value in the eyes of your admirer, and make it less possible for you to avoid the notice of the world. A liaison of this kind ought to be free from all ill effects, and an advantage to both parties. I think that I have said enough, but if I have omitted any point that you would like me to touch on, by all means ask me.'

INTERLUDE

PHAEDRUS: Well, what do you think of the speech, Socrates? Isn't it a wonderful piece of work, especially the diction?

SOCRATES: More than wonderful, my friend, divine; it quite took my breath away. It is you who are responsible for this effect on me, Phaedrus. I concentrated on you and saw how what you were reading put you in a glow; so, believing that you know more about these things than I do, I followed your example and joined in the ecstasy, you inspired man.

PHAEDRUS: Do you think that this is a laughing matter?

SOCRATES: Why, don't you think I'm serious?

PHAEDRUS: Don't talk like that, Socrates. But tell me seriously, in the name of friendship, do you think that there is another man in Greece who could produce a grander and fuller discourse on this subject than what we have heard?

SOCRATES: Well, must our approval of the speech extend to its matter, or may we confine ourselves to admiring the clarity and shapeliness and precision with which every phrase is turned? If the former, it is you who must take the responsibility. I am such an idiot that I let it pass me by and attended only to the style; the matter I didn't suppose that even Lysias himself could think satisfactory. I submit to your better judgement, Phaedrus, but it seems to me that he has said the same things two or three times over, either because he could not find sufficient matter to produce variety on a single topic, or perhaps from sheer lack of interest in the subject. The speech struck me as a piece of youthful exhibitionism; an attempt to demonstrate how he could say the same thing in two different ways, each as good as the other.

PHAEDRUS: Nonsense, Socrates. If the speech has one merit above all others, it is that no single aspect of the subject worth mentioning has been omitted; no one could improve on it either in fullness or quality.

SOCRATES: Here I can go along with you no further. If I give way, to please you, wise men and women of old who have spoken and written on the subject will prove me wrong.

PHAEDRUS: Who are they? And where have you heard it better treated?

SOCRATES: I can't tell you off-hand, but certainly by someone, either lovely Sappho or wise Anacreon or some prose writers. I am sure of this because my own heart is full and I have a feeling that I could compose a different speech not inferior to this. Now I am far too well aware of my own ignorance to suppose that any of these ideas can be my own. The explanation must be that I have been filled from some external source, like a jar from a spring, but I am such a fool that I have forgotten how or from whom.

PHAEDRUS: My good friend, you never said a better word. Never mind how or from whom – don't tell me even if I ask you – just do what you've said; provide me with another speech better and equally full, avoiding the arguments already used. I promise I'll do like the nine archons, and set up at Delphi a life-size image in gold of you as well as of myself.

SOCRATES: You are a dear fellow, Phaedrus, genuine gold all through, if you suppose me to mean that Lysias has completely missed the mark, and that it is possible to compose a second entirely different speech. That could hardly be true even of the feeblest writer. Take the thesis of his speech to begin with; if one is arguing that the non-lover is to be preferred to the lover, how can one avoid taking the obvious line of praising the good sense of the former and censuring the folly of the latter? No, we must not find fault with commonplaces of that sort; their use must be allowed and treated with forbearance, though it is only by their skilful arrangement and not by their originality that they can earn praise; whereas less obvious and more recondite ideas are to be commended for their novelty as well as for their neat use.

PHAEDRUS: I concede your point, which seems very reasonable. I will let you take for granted that the lover is in a less healthy state than the non-lover, and if you can produce a speech which is otherwise different from Lysias' and more copious and convincing as well, you shall stand in wrought gold at Olympia beside the offering of the Cypselids.

SOCRATES: Are you taking me seriously, Phaedrus, because by way of teasing you I made an attack on your favourite? Do you think that I shall make a serious attempt to outdo the clever Lysias by something more subtle?

PHAEDRUS: If it comes to that, my friend, you have laid yourself open to the same treatment as you gave me. Unless we are to indulge in an exchange of the sort of vulgar repartee that occurs in comedies, you had better deliver your speech to the best of your ability. Don't drive me to say: 'Socrates, I know Socrates as well as I know my own name; he was longing to speak but he was coy.' Take it from me that we are not going to leave this spot till you have uttered what you said you had in mind. We are alone and I am younger and stronger than you, so mark my words and don't compel me to use force to get what you may as well supply without reluctance.

SOCRATES: But, my good Phaedrus, it would be ludicrous for a layman like myself to extemporize on a subject which has been already treated by a good writer.

PHAEDRUS: You know the situation, so stop playing with me. Anyhow, I fancy that I can say something which will make you speak.

SOCRATES: Then don't say it.

PHAEDRUS: I certainly shall. Here it is and it takes the form of an oath. I swear to you by — what god shall I invoke? Or shall it be this plane tree? Yes; I swear by this tree that unless you deliver your speech in its actual presence I will never give you sight or word of another speech by anybody.

SOCRATES: Oh, you wretch, what a splendid device for making a man who loves speeches do what you want.

PHAEDRUS: Then why go on shuffling?

SOCRATES: Since you have taken this oath, I won't. I can't cut myself off from that kind of entertainment.

PHAEDRUS: Speak on then.

SOCRATES: Shall I tell you what I'll do?

PHAEDRUS: What?

SOCRATES: I'll speak with my face covered. In that way I shall get through the speech most quickly, and I shan't be put out by catching your eye and feeling ashamed.

PHAEDRUS: You may do what you like if you'll only begin.

SOCRATES' FIRST SPEECH

SOCRATES: Come then, shrill Muses, whether it be to the character of your song or to the tuneful race of Ligurians that ye owe your name of shrill, help me in the tale which this fine gentleman is forcing me to tell, in order that his friend, whom he already thinks so brilliant, may seem to him hereafter even more brilliant than before.

Once upon a time there was a boy, or rather a lad, who was exceedingly handsome. Among his many admirers there was one subtle person, no less in love than the rest, who had, however, persuaded the lad that he was not in love with him. And once in the course of his suit he was trying to convince him that a man not in love has a better claim to be favoured than a lover. His argument was as follows:

In every discussion, my dear boy, there is one and only one way of beginning if one is to come to a sound conclusion; that is to know what it is that one is discussing; otherwise one is bound entirely to miss the mark. Now most people are unaware that they are ignorant of the essential nature of their subject, whatever it may be. Believing that they know it, they do not begin their discussion by agreeing about the use of terms, with the natural result that as they proceed they fall into self-contradictions and misunderstandings. Do not let us make the mistake for which we find fault with others. The subject that we are discussing is whether the friendship of a lover or of a non-lover is preferable. Let us begin then by agreeing upon a definition of the nature and power of love, and keep this before our eyes to refer to as we debate whether love does good or harm.

Love is a kind of desire – everyone will admit that – but we know that one does not have to be in love to desire what is beautiful. How then are we to distinguish between a lover and his opposite? We must realize that in each one of us there are two ruling and impelling principles whose guidance we follow, a desire for pleasure, which is innate, and an acquired conviction which causes us to aim at excellence. These two principles are sometimes in agreement within us and sometimes at variance; at one moment the first and at another the second prevails. The conviction which impels us towards excellence is rational, and the power by which it masters us we call self-control; the desire which drags us towards pleasure is irrational, and when it gets the upper hand in us its dominion is called excess. Excess has many categories and takes many forms and goes by a variety of names. Whichever of these forms is most in evidence confers upon its possessor its own peculiar name, an acquisition which is far from being honourable or valuable. If, for example, the desire which prevails over sound reason and all the other desires is concerned with food, it is called gluttony, and its possessor will receive the corresponding name of glutton; if on the other hand the desire which gains absolute sway and leads its possessor down its own particular path is desire for drink, we do not need to be told what he will be called; and similarly with the kindred desires and their names: whichever of them happens at any moment to be dominant, we are left in no doubt of the appropriate name. The conclusion to which all this is leading is obvious, but for the sake of clarity it is better to be quite explicit. When the irrational desire that prevails over the conviction which aims at right is directed at the pleasure derived from beauty, and in the case of physical beauty powerfully reinforced by the appetites which are akin to it, so that it emerges victorious, it takes its name from the very power with which it is endowed and is called *eros* or passionate love.

Tell me, my dear Phaedrus, do you think, as I do, that I am inspired?

PHAEDRUS: Undoubtedly you have been carried away by a quite unusual flow of eloquence, Socrates.

SOCRATES: Be quiet then and listen. This spot seems full of spirits, so do not be surprised if, as my speech goes on, the nymphs take possession of me. In fact, what I am uttering now is almost lyrical.

PHAEDRUS: Very true.

SOCRATES: *You* are responsible for this. But listen to what remains; perhaps the madness that is coming upon me may yet be averted. We must leave that to God; our business is to resume the argument addressed to the lad.

Well then, my good fellow, we have defined in words the subject of our discussion. With this in mind let us go on to the further question of what good or harm is likely to result from the lover and the non-lover respectively to the person who yields to them.

The man who is under the sway of desire and a slave to pleasure will inevitably try to derive the greatest pleasure possible from the object of his passion. Now a man in a morbid state finds pleasure in complete absence of opposition, and detests any appearance of superiority or equality in his darling; he will always do his best to keep him in a state of inferiority and subservience. Seeing therefore that an ignoramus is inferior to a wise man, a coward to a hero, a poor speaker to a man of eloquence, a slow mind to a quick wit, a lover will inevitably be delighted if he finds these and a number of other mental defects part of the natural endowment of his beloved, or will do his best to foster them if they are in the course of being acquired; otherwise he must lose the prospect of immediate enjoyment. Moreover, he will of course be jealous, and by keeping his favourite from the kind of society most likely to help him to become a man he will do him great harm. The worst form that this harm can take is deprivation of what would make him most intelligent, that is to say of divine philosophy; a lover is bound to keep him away from this for fear of incurring his contempt, and generally speaking to do everything in his power to ensure that he shall be totally ignorant and totally dependent upon the lover, a state in which he will give the greatest pleasure to his admirer and inflict the greatest injury upon himself. So, as far as his mind is concerned, he cannot have a less desirable protector or companion than a man who is in love with him.

Next consider what kind of physical condition the man who is forced to pursue pleasure rather than good will hope to find or will encourage in anyone whom he gets into his power. The person we shall see him running after will be soft rather than tough, the product of a breeding in chequered shade rather than clear sunshine, a stranger to manly toil and honest sweat, accustomed to luxurious and effeminate living, supplying his natural deficiency of complexion by the use of cosmetics, and indulging in all the other practices that go with these characteristics. We know what they are; there is no need to pursue the matter further; we can sum up in a single phrase and pass on. In war or any other great emergency a physical condition such as I have described inspires as much confidence in the enemy as fear in one's own side and even in one's lovers themselves.

So much is obvious and we can proceed to the next point – how will the society and protection of a lover affect one's material circumstances for good or harm? Everyone knows, and the lover above all, that he would like his favourite to be devoid of the dearest and kindest and most perfect belongings that a man can have; he would be quite happy for him to be without father or mother or kindred or friends, because their disapproval is likely to prevent him from deriving the highest enjoyment from the liaison. As for property in cash or in any other form, the existence of this will in his opinion make the pursuit more difficult, and the pursued less easy to handle even when he is in the toils. The lover, then, will inevitably grudge his favourite the possession of wealth and be glad when he loses it. In addition, he will naturally pray that his beloved should remain wifeless, childless, and homeless for as long as possible, because he wants to enjoy the sweets of possession for the longest possible time.

Many other things which are bad in themselves nevertheless by some dispensation of providence have a momentary pleasure attached to them. A toady, for instance, is a dreadful animal and does much harm, yet the ready wit which nature has implanted in him is a source of pleasure. The trade of a prostitute is mischievous and one may condemn such creatures and their activities, yet the enjoyment that they afford is very sweet while it lasts. But the companionship of a lover, besides being injurious, is in the highest degree disagreeable to the object of his passion. Like to like, as the old proverb says; equals in age have the same pleasures, and this similarity begets friendship; but the society even of one's contemporaries palls in the end. Besides, every kind of constraint is felt to be a burden, and that is precisely what a lover imposes on his darling in addition to their discrepancy of age. He is old and his companion is young, yet he never leaves his side day or night if he can help it; he is driven on by an irresistible itch to the pleasures which are constantly to be found in seeing, hearing, and touching his beloved, in fact in every sensation which makes him conscious of his presence; no wonder then that he takes delight in close attendance on him. But what compensating pleasures are there for the other party to prevent a companionship of such length ending in utter distaste? Before his eyes is a man older than himself and no longer in his first youth, with all the defects that go with advancing years, defects which it is disagreeable even to hear of, far more to come into physical contact with under the pressure of a necessity which never relaxes. Worse still, he is the object of jealous vigilance at all times and in all company; he has to listen to unseasonable and excessive praise of himself, or else to reproaches which are hard to bear even when the lover is sober, but which when he is drunk are disgraceful as well as intolerable, owing to the disgusting and unreserved freedom with which they are uttered.

While he is in love the lover is a tedious nuisance, but when his passion cools you can place no reliance on him for the future, in spite of all the promises which he mixed with his oaths and entreaties in order to maintain, through the expectation of benefits to come, a precarious hold upon an intimacy which even then the beloved found irksome. When the time comes to pay his debts he is under the sway of a new influence; rational self-control has replaced the madness of love; he is a different man and has forgotten his darling. So when the latter treats him as if he were still the same, and reminds him of what he did and said, and asks him to requite the favours he has received, he is ashamed to say that he has changed, but does not know how to fulfil the oaths and promises which he made when he was the slave of irrational passion. Now that he has come to his senses and regained his self-control he has no wish to behave as he did in the past and thus to relapse into his former condition. So the sometime lover has no choice but to escape his creditor by flight; the other side of the coin has come uppermost now, and it is his turn to run away, while his former favourite is forced to pursue him with angry reproaches, all because he did not realize at the start that it is far better to yield to a non-lover who is in his sober senses than to a lover who from the very nature of things is bound to be out of his mind. The alternative is to put oneself in the power of a man who is faithless, morose, jealous, and disagreeable, who will do harm to one's estate, harm to one's physical health, and harm above all to one's spiritual development, than which nothing is or ever will be more precious in the sight of God and man. Take this to heart then, my lad, and learn the lesson that there is no kindness in the friendship of a lover; its object is the satisfaction of an appetite, like the appetite for food. 'As wolves for lambs, so lovers lust for boys.'

SOCRATES: I told you how it would be, Phaedrus; you shan't hear another word from me. Make no mistake about it; my speech is over.

PHAEDRUS: But I thought you were only half way, and I was expecting you to balance what you have said already by describing the advantages to be derived from yielding to the man who is not in love. Why are you stopping at this point, Socrates?

SOCRATES: Haven't you noticed, bless you, that I have become not merely lyrical but actually epic, as if the former weren't bad enough? If I embark on a eulogy of the second type, what do you think will happen to me? These nymphs, to whose influence you meant to expose me all along, will drive me positively beside myself. Anyhow, there's no need for a long harangue: I've already said enough about both types; simply take the opposites of all the bad qualities I attributed to the first and confer them on the second. My tale must meet with whatever fate it deserves; I shall cross the stream and go away, before you exercise some stronger compulsion on me.

PHAEDRUS: Don't go till the heat of the day is over, Socrates. Look, it's almost high noon already, and the sun is at its strongest. Let us stay here and discuss what we have heard and go away presently when it gets cool.

SOCRATES: Your passion for rhetoric, Phaedrus, is super-human, simply amazing. I really believe that no one in your lifetime has been responsible for the production of more speeches than you, if we include besides those you deliver yourself those you somehow compel other people to deliver.

Simmias of Thebes is an exception, but you beat the rest easily. And now it looks as if you have given occasion for yet another discourse from me.

PHAEDRUS: That's anything but a declaration of war. But tell me what you mean.

SOCRATES: Just as I was about to cross the stream, Phaedrus, I received the supernatural sign which sometimes comes to me – every time it happens it restrains me from doing what I am about to do – and I seemed suddenly to hear a voice declaring that I had committed a sin and must not go away till I had expiated it. My powers of divination are only slight – in fact, I am like those readers who can just pick out their letters – but they are just sufficient for my own concerns. I see clearly now where my offence lies, for the soul itself is endowed with some power of divination. Even while I was speaking some time ago I felt a certain uneasiness; in the words of Ibycus, I was afraid that I might be 'purchasing honour with men at the price of offending the gods'. Now I see where I went wrong.

PHAEDRUS: Where?

SOCRATES: Our speeches were dreadful, Phaedrus, dreadful, both the speech you brought with you and the speech you made me utter.

PHAEDRUS: In what way?

SOCRATES: They were silly and more than a little blasphemous. What could be worse than that?

PHAEDRUS: Nothing, if what you say is true.

SOCRATES: Well, don't you believe that Love is the son of Aphrodite and a god?

PHAEDRUS: So we are told.

SOCRATES: That is not how he was spoken of by Lysias, or in

23

that speech of yours, which came out of my lips because you put a spell on them. If Love is a god, or at any rate a being with something divine about him, as he certainly is, he cannot be evil, but both our recent speeches represented him as being so. In that way both sinned against Love. What could be more exquisitely silly than for them to give themselves airs for the approval they could win by imposing on a few feeble mortals, when they did not contain a single sound or true idea? So then, my friend, I must purge my offence. For those who make mistakes in mythology there is an old remedy, which Stesichorus was aware of, though Homer was not. When he lost his sight for speaking ill of Helen, Stesichorus, unlike Homer, was sagacious enough to understand the reason; he immediately composed the poem which begins:

> False is this tale. You never
> Went in a ship to sea,
> Nor saw the towers of Troy.

And as soon as he had finished what is called his palinode or recantation he recovered his sight. Now I propose to be even cleverer than our forebears; I mean to deliver a palinode to Love before I suffer any harm for the wrong I have done him, and I will deliver it with my head uncovered, not muffling myself up from bashfulness as I did before.

PHAEDRUS: Nothing you could have said would give me greater pleasure, Socrates.

SOCRATES: That, my good Phaedrus, is because you realize the irreverence of those two speeches, mine just now and the one you read from your manuscript. Anyone of good birth and breeding, in love with someone of like nature, or himself previously the object of love, who heard us saying that lovers conceive great hatreds for trivial reasons and behave jealously and injuriously to those they love, so far from agreeing with us in our aspersions on Love, would think that he was listening to men brought up among the scum of a sea-port, who had never seen what love between freeborn men was like.

PHAEDRUS: Perhaps you are right, Socrates.

SOCRATES: The thought of such a man makes me ashamed, and Love himself fills me with dread. So I am anxious to wash the brine out of my ears, so to speak, with the fresh water of some sound doctrine. And I advise Lysias, too, to lose no time in writing a speech to the effect that, other things being equal, one ought to favour a lover rather than a non-lover.

PHAEDRUS: You need have no fear about that. Once you have spoken on the side of the lover I shall absolutely compel Lysias to write a speech on the same subject.

SOCRATES: I feel sure of it, as long as you remain the man you are.

PHAEDRUS: Speak on then.

SOCRATES: Where is the lad I was addressing? I want him to hear this too, before for lack of it he falls into the error of yielding to the non-lover.

PHAEDRUS: He is always here at your elbow, whenever you need him.

SOCRATES' SECOND SPEECH
TYPES OF DIVINE MADNESS. THE IMMORTALITY
OF SOUL.

SOCRATES: Well then, my handsome lad, you must realize that the previous speech was the work of Phaedrus, son of

Pythocles, a man of Myrrhinus, whereas this which you are about to hear comes from Stesichorus, son of Euphemus, a native of Himera. This is how it must go. False is the tale which says that because the lover is mad and the non-lover sane the non-lover should be given the preference when one might have a lover. If it were true without qualification that madness is an evil, that would be all very well, but in fact madness, provided it comes as the gift of heaven, is the channel by which we receive the greatest blessings. Take the prophetess at Delphi and the priestesses at Dodona, for example, and consider all the benefits which individuals and states in Greece have received from them when they were in a state of frenzy, though their usefulness in their sober senses amounts to little or nothing. And if we were to include the Sibyl and others who by the use of inspired divination have set many inquirers on the right track about the future, we should be telling at tedious length what everyone knows. But this at least is worth pointing out, that the men of old who gave things their names saw no disgrace or reproach in madness; otherwise they would not have connected with it the name of the noblest of all arts, the art of discerning the future, and called it the *manic* art. The fact that they did so shows that they looked upon madness as a fine thing, when it comes upon a man by divine dispensation, but their successors have bungled matters by the introduction of a T and produced the word *mantic*. Similarly, augury and the other methods by which men in their right minds inquire into the future, and through which they acquire insight and information by the exercise of purely human thought, were originally called *oiŏnoistic*, but later generations by lengthening the O to make it sound impressive have brought it into connection with birds (*oi-ōnoi*), and called it *oiōnistic*. So, according to the evidence provided by our ancestors, madness is a nobler thing than sober sense, in proportion as the name of the mantic art and the act it signifies are more perfect and held in higher esteem than the name and act of augury; madness comes from God, whereas sober sense is merely human.

In the next place, when ancient sins have given rise to severe maladies and troubles, which have afflicted the members of certain families, madness has appeared among them and by breaking forth into prophecy has brought relief by the appropriate means: by recourse, that is to say, to prayer and worship. It has discovered in rites of purification and initiation a way to make the sufferer well and to keep him well thereafter, and has provided for the man whose madness and possession were of the right type a way of escape from the evils that beset him.

The third type of possession and madness is possession by the Muses. When this seizes upon a gentle and virgin soul it rouses it to inspired expression in lyric and other sorts of poetry, and glorifies countless deeds of the heroes of old for the instruction of posterity. But if a man comes to the door of poetry untouched by the madness of the Muses, believing that technique alone will make him a good poet, he and his sane compositions never reach perfection, but are utterly eclipsed by the performances of the inspired madman.

These are but some examples of the noble effect of heaven-sent madness. Intrinsically there is nothing in it to frighten us, and we must not allow ourselves to be alarmed and upset by those who say that the friendship of a man in his sober senses is preferable to that of one whose mind is disturbed. They will prove their case only if they can demonstrate in addition that love sent from heaven is not a blessing to lover and loved alike. It is for us to prove the opposite, and to show that this type of madness is the greatest benefit that heaven can confer on us. Our argument will carry conviction with the wise, though not with the merely clever. First of all we must form a true notion of the nature of soul, divine and human, by observing it in both its passive and its active aspects. And the first step in our demonstration is this.

All soul is immortal; for what is always in motion is immortal. But that which owes its motion to something else, even though it is itself the cause of motion in another thing, may cease to be in motion and therefore cease to live. Only what moves itself never ceases to be in motion, since it could not so cease without being false to its own nature; it is the source and prime origin of movement in all other things that move. Now a prime origin cannot come into being; all that comes into being must derive its existence from a prime origin, but the prime origin itself derives from nothing; for if a prime origin were derived from anything, it would no longer be a prime origin.

Moreover, since it does not come into being, it must also be indestructible; for since all things must be derived from a prime origin, if the prime origin is destroyed, it will not come into being again out of anything, nor any other thing out of it. So we see that the prime origin of motion is what moves itself, and this can neither be destroyed nor come into being: otherwise the whole universe and the whole creation would collapse and come to a stop, and there would be nothing by which it could again be set in motion and come into existence. Now, since it has been proved that what moves itself is immortal, a man need feel no hesitation in identifying it with the essence and definition of soul. For all body which has its source of motion outside itself is soulless; but a body which moves itself from within is endowed with soul, since self-motion is of the very nature of soul. If then it is established that what moves itself is identical with soul, it inevitably follows that soul is uncreated and immortal.

THE MYTH. THE ALLEGORY OF THE CHARIOTEER
AND HIS HORSES. THE PROCESSION OF THE
GODS AND THE VISION OF REALITY. THE
FALL, INCARNATION AND LIBERATION OF THE
SOUL. THE PRIVILEGE OF THE PHILOSOPHER.
RECOLLECTION AS A MEANS TO THE RECAPTURE
OF KNOWLEDGE OF THE FORMS.

SOCRATES: This must suffice concerning soul's immortality; concerning its nature we must give the following account. To describe it as it is would require a long exposition of which only a god is capable; but it is within the power of man to say in shorter compass what it resembles. Let us adopt this method, and compare the soul to a winged charioteer and his team acting together. Now all the horses and charioteers of the gods are good and come of good stock, but in other beings there is a mixture of good and bad. First of all we must make it plain that the ruling power in us men drives a pair of horses, and next that one of these horses is fine and good and of noble stock, and the other the opposite in every way. So in our case the task of the charioteer is necessarily a difficult and unpleasant business.

Now we must try to tell how it is that we speak of both

mortal and immortal living beings. Soul taken as a whole is in charge of all that is inanimate, and traverses the entire universe, appearing at different times in different forms. When it is perfect and winged it moves on high and governs all creation, but the soul that has shed its wings falls until it encounters solid matter. There it settles and puts on an earthly body, which appears to be self-moving because of the power of soul that is in it, and this combination of soul and body is given the name of a living being and is termed mortal. There is not a single sound reason for positing the existence of such a being who is immortal, but because we have never seen or formed an adequate idea of a god, we picture him to ourselves as a being of the same kind as ourselves but immortal, a combination of soul and body indissolubly joined for ever. The existence of such beings and the use of such language about them we must leave to the will of God; let us pass on to consider the reason which causes a soul to shed and lose its wings; it is something like this.

The function of a wing is to take what is heavy and raise it up into the region above, where the gods dwell; of all things connected with the body, it has the greatest affinity with the divine, which is endowed with beauty, wisdom, goodness and every other excellence. These qualities are the prime source of nourishment and growth to the wings of the soul, but their opposites, such as ugliness and evil, cause the wings to waste and perish. Behold, first in the procession, driving his winged team, goes Zeus the mighty leader of the heavenly array, whose providence orders and watches over all things. There follows him a host of gods and spirits marshalled in eleven bands; for Hestia alone remains behind in the house of the gods, while the rest of the twelve ruler gods lead on their companies, each in the station which is appointed for him. Now many glorious sights meet the eyes of the blessed gods on the journeys to and fro beneath the vault of heaven which they take in pursuit, each of his allotted task, and they are followed by whoever is able and willing to follow them, since jealousy has no place in the company of the divine. But when they go to the celebration of their high feast day, they take the steep path leading to the summit of the arch which supports the outer heaven. The teams of the gods, which are well matched and tractable, go easily, but the rest go with difficulty; for the horse with the vicious nature, if he has not been well broken in, drags his driver down by throwing all his weight in the direction of the earth; supreme then is the agony of the struggle which awaits the soul.

Now the souls that are termed immortal, when they reach the summit of the arch, go outside the vault and stand upon the back of the universe; standing there they are carried round by its revolution while they contemplate what lies outside the heavens. But of this region beyond the skies no mortal poet has sung or ever will sing in such strains as it deserves. Nevertheless the fact is this; for we must have the courage to speak the truth, especially when truth itself is our theme. The region of which I speak is the abode of the reality with which true knowledge is concerned, a reality without colour or shape, intangible but utterly real, apprehensible only by intellect which is the pilot of the soul. So the mind of a god, sustained as it is by pure intelligence and knowledge, like that of every soul which is destined to assimilate its proper food, is satisfied at last with the vision of reality, and nourished and made happy by the contemplation of truth, until the circular revolution brings it back to its starting-point. And in the course of its journey it beholds absolute justice and discipline and knowledge, not the knowledge which is attached to things which come into being, nor the knowledge which varies with the objects which we now call real, but the absolute knowledge which corresponds to what is absolutely real in the fullest sense. And when in like manner it has beheld and taken its fill of the other objects which constitute absolute reality, it withdraws again within the vault of heaven and goes home. And when it comes home the charioteer sets his horses at their manger and puts ambrosia before them and with it a draught of nectar to drink.

Such is the life of the gods. But of the other souls that which is likest to a god and best able to follow keeps the head of its charioteer above the surface as it makes the circuit, though the unruly behaviour of its horses impairs its vision of reality. A second class sometimes rises and sometimes sinks, and owing to the restiveness of its horses sees part, but not the whole. The rest, in spite of their unanimous striving to reach the upper world, fail to do so, and are carried round beneath the surface, trampling and jostling one another, each eager to outstrip its neighbour. Great is the confusion and struggle and sweat, and many souls are lamed and many have their wings all broken through the feebleness of their charioteers; finally, for all their toil, they depart without achieving initiation into the vision of reality, and feed henceforth upon mere opinion.

The reason for their extreme eagerness to behold the plain of truth is that the meadow there produces fit pasturage for the best part of the soul, and that the wings by which the soul is borne aloft are nourished by it. And it is decreed by fate that any soul which has attained some vision of truth by following in the train of a god shall remain unscathed till the next great circuit, and if it can continue thus for ever shall be for ever free from hurt. But when a soul fails to follow and misses the vision, and as the result of some mishap sinks beneath its burden of forgetfulness and wrongdoing, so that it loses its wings and falls to earth, the law is this. In its first incarnation no soul is born in the likeness of a beast; the soul that has seen the most enters into a human infant who is destined to become a seeker after wisdom or beauty or a follower of the Muses and a lover; the next most perceptive is born as a law-abiding monarch or as a warrior and commander; the third as a man of affairs or the manager of a household or a financier; the fourth is to be a lover of physical activity or a trainer or physician; the fifth is given the life of a soothsayer or an official of the mysteries; the sixth will make a poet or a practitioner of some other imitative art; the seventh an artisan or a farmer; the eighth a popular teacher or a demagogue; the ninth a tyrant.

In all this the lot which befalls a man between two incarnations corresponds to the goodness or badness of his previous life. The individual soul does not return whence it came for ten thousand years; so long does it take for a soul to grow its wings again, except it be the soul of one who has sought after wisdom without guile or whose love for a boy has been combined with such a search. These souls, if they choose the life of the philosopher three times successively, regain their wings in the third period of a thousand years, and in the three-thousandth year win their release. The rest at the end of their first life are brought to judgement, and after judgement some go to expiate their sins in places of punishment beneath the earth, while others are borne aloft by justice to a certain region of the heavens to enjoy the reward which their previous life in human form has earned. But in the thousandth year both sorts alike must draw lots and make choice of their second life, each soul according to its own pleasure. At this moment a human soul may take upon itself the life of a beast, or a soul which was originally human may change from beast back to man. It is impossible for a soul that has never seen the truth to enter into our human shape; it takes a man to understand by the use of universals, and to collect out of the multiplicity of sense-impressions a unity arrived at by a process of reason. Such a process is simply the recollection of the things which our soul once perceived when it took its journey with a god, looking down from above on the things to which we now ascribe reality and gazing upwards towards what is truly real. That is why it is right that the soul of the philosopher alone should regain its wings; for it is always dwelling in memory as best it may upon those things which a god owes his divinity to dwelling upon. It is only by the right use of such aids to recollection, which form a continual initiation into the perfect mystic vision that a man can become perfect in the true sense of the word. Because he stands apart from the common objects of human ambition and applies himself to the divine, he is reproached by most men for being out of his wits; they do not realize that he is in fact possessed by a god.

This then is the fourth type of madness, which befalls when a man, reminded by the sight of beauty on earth of the true beauty, grows his wings and endeavours to fly upwards, but in vain, exposing himself to the reproach of insanity because like a bird he fixes his gaze on the heights to the neglect of things below; and the conclusion to which our whole discourse points is that in itself and in its origin this is the best of all forms of divine possession, both for the subject himself and for his associate, and it is when he is touched with this madness that the man whose love is aroused by beauty in others is called a lover. As I have said, every human soul by its very nature has beheld true being – otherwise it would not have entered into the creature we call man – but it is not every soul that finds it easy to use its present experience as a means of recollecting the world of reality. Some had but a brief glimpse of the truth in their former existence; others have been so unfortunate as to be corrupted by evil associations since they fell to earth, with the result that they have forgotten the sacred vision they once saw. Few are left who retain a sufficient memory. These, however, when they see some likeness of the world above, are beside themselves and lose all control, but do not realize what is happening to them because of the dimness of their perceptions.

Now the earthly likenesses of justice and self-discipline and all the other forms which are precious to souls keep no lustre, and there are few who by the use of their feeble faculties and with great difficulty can recognize in the counterfeits the family likeness of the originals. But beauty was once ours to see in all its brightness, when in the company of the blessed we followed Zeus as others followed some other of the Olympians, to enjoy the beatific vision and to be initiated into that mystery which brings, we may say with reverence, supreme felicity. Whole were we who celebrated that festival, unspotted by all the evils which awaited us in time to come, and whole and unspotted and changeless and serene were the objects revealed to us in the light of that mystic vision. Pure was the light and pure were we from the pollution of the walking sepulchre which we call a body, to which we are bound like an oyster to its shell.

LOVE IS THE REGROWTH OF THE WINGS OF THE SOUL. THE DIFFERENT TYPES OF LOVER.

SOCRATES: So much by way of tribute to memory, whose revival of our yearning for the past has led us far afield. But beauty, as we were saying, shone bright in the world above, and here too it still gleams clearest, even as the sense by which we apprehend it is our clearest. For sight is the keenest of our physical senses, though it does not bring us knowledge. What overpowering love knowledge would inspire if it could bring as clear an image of itself before our sight, and the same may be said of the other forms which are fitted to arouse love. But as things are it is only beauty which has the privilege of being both the most clearly discerned and the most lovely. Now the man who is not fresh from his initiation or who has been corrupted does not quickly make the transition from beauty on earth to absolute beauty; so when he sees its namesake here he feels no reverence for it, but surrenders himself to sensuality and is eager like a four-footed beast to mate and to beget children, or in his addiction to wantonness feels no fear or shame in pursuing a pleasure which is unnatural. But the newly initiated, who has had a full sight of the celestial vision, when he beholds a god-like face or a physical form which truly reflects ideal beauty, first of all shivers and experiences something of the dread which the vision itself inspired; next he gazes upon it and worships it as if it were a god, and, if he were not afraid of being thought an utter madman, he would sacrifice to his beloved as to the image of a divinity. Then, as you would expect after a cold fit, his condition changes and he falls into an unaccustomed sweat; he receives through his eyes the emanation of beauty, by which the soul's plumage is fostered, and grows hot, and this heat is accompanied by a softening of the passages from which the feathers grow, passages which have long been parched and closed up, so as to prevent any feathers from shooting. As the nourishing moisture falls upon it the stump of each feather under the whole surface of the soul swells and strives to grow from its root; for in its original state the soul was feathered all over. So now it is all in a state of ferment and throbbing; in fact the soul of a man who is beginning to grow his feathers has the same sensations of pricking and irritation and itching as children feel in their gums when they are just beginning to cut their teeth.

When in this condition the soul gazes upon the beauty of its beloved, and is fostered and warmed by the emanations which flood in upon it – which is why we speak of a 'flood' of longing – it wins relief from its pain and is glad; but when it is parched by separation the openings of the passages where the feathers shoot close up through drought and obstruct the development of the new growth. Imprisoned below the surface together with the flood of longing of which I have spoken, each embryo feather throbs like a pulse and presses against its proper outlet, so that the soul is driven mad by the pain of the pricks in every part, and yet feels gladness because it preserves the memory of the beauty of its darling. In this state of mingled pleasure and pain the sufferer is perplexed by the strangeness of his experience and struggles helplessly; in his frenzy he cannot sleep at night or remain still by day, but his longing drives him wherever he thinks that he may see the possessor of beauty. When he sees him and his soul is refreshed by the flood of emanations the closed passages are unstopped; he obtains a respite from his pains and pangs, and there is nothing to equal the sweetness of the pleasure which he enjoys for the moment. From this state he never willingly emerges; in his eyes no one can compare with his beloved; mother, brothers, friends, all are forgotten, and if his property is lost through his negligence he thinks nothing of it; the conventions of civilized behaviour, on whose observance he used to pride himself, he now scorns; he is ready to be a slave and to make his bed as near as he is allowed to the object of his passion; for besides the reverence which he feels for the possessor of beauty he has found in him the only physician for sickness of the most grievous kind. This sickness, let me inform the handsome lad whom I am supposed to be addressing, men call *eros*, but the gods have a name for it which in his youthful ignorance he will probably laugh at. There are two lines on love quoted by the admirers of Homer from the apocryphal works, of which the second is highly bizarre and not free from defects of metre. They go as follows:

Eros the god that flies is his name in the language of mortals:
But from the wings he must grow he is called by celestials Pteros.

You may believe this or not as you like, but the cause and the effect of what happens to lovers are as I have described.
The burden imposed by the god who takes his name from wings is borne with greater dignity if the bearer be one who followed in the train of Zeus. But those who attached themselves to Ares and made the circuit with him, if they fall a prey to love and conceive themselves to be injured by the

object of their passion, thirst for blood and are ready to sacrifice both their own lives and their favourite's. Similarly with the other gods; every man during his first incarnation on earth, as long as he remains uncorrupted, spends his time in worshipping and doing his best to imitate the particular god whose devotee he was, and conducts himself accordingly in his dealings with those he loves and with the rest of the world. So in selecting his love from among the possessors of beauty each man follows his own bent, and, treating his beloved as if he were himself a god, he fashions and adorns an image, metaphorically speaking, and makes it the object of his honour and worship. Now those who were followers of Zeus desire a Zeus-like disposition in the person they are to love; they look for a temperament in which love of wisdom is combined with ability to lead, and when they find it they fall in love and do everything in their power to encourage its natural tendency. If they have not previously embarked on this pursuit, they now apply themselves to the discovery of truth from every available source of knowledge and from their own personal researches; they find in themselves traces by which they can detect the nature of the god to whom they belong, and their task is facilitated by the necessity which constrains them to keep their eyes fixed upon him; by the aid of memory they lay hold of him and are possessed by him, so that they take from him their character and their way of life, in so far as it is possible for a man to partake of divinity. Believing that their beloved is the cause of this they cherish him all the more, and whatever draughts of inspiration they draw from Zeus they pour out like Bacchants over the soul of their darling, and so make him as like as possible to the god they serve. Those who follow in the train of Hera look for a kingly disposition in the object of their choice, and when they find it act towards it in every respect like the followers of Zeus. And so with the followers of Apollo and of each of the other gods: every man desires to find in his favourite a nature comparable to his own particular divinity, and when he lights upon such a one he devotes himself to personal imitation of his god and at the same time attempts to persuade and train his beloved to the best of his power to walk in the ways of that god and to mould himself upon him. There is no room for jealousy or mean spite; his whole effort is concentrated upon leading the object of his love into the closest possible conformity with himself and with the god he worships. This is the aspiration of the true lover, and this, if he succeeds in gaining his object in the way I describe, is the glorious and happy initiation which befalls the beloved when his affections are captured by a friend whom love has made mad. Now the manner of his capture is this.

THE CHARIOTEER ALLEGORY RESUMED. THE
SUBJUGATION OF APPETITE, TYPIFIED BY THE
BAD HORSE, AND THE AWAKENING OF LOVE
FOR THE LOVER IN THE BELOVED. A CONCLUDING
PRAYER TO THE GOD FOR LYSIAS AND PHAEDRUS.

SOCRATES: Let us abide by the distinction we drew at the beginning of our story, when we divided each soul into three elements, and compared two of them to horses and the third to their charioteer. One of the horses, we say, is good and one not; but we did not go fully into the excellence of the good or the badness of the vicious horse, and that is what we must now do. The horse that is harnessed on the senior side is upright and clean-limbed; he holds his neck high and has a somewhat hooked nose; his colour is white, with black eyes; his thirst for honour is tempered by restraint and modesty; he is a friend to genuine renown and needs no whip, but is driven simply by the word of command. The other horse is crooked, lumbering, ill-made; stiff-necked, short-throated, snub-nosed; his coat is black and his eyes a bloodshot grey; wantonness and boastfulness are his companions, and he is hairy-eared and deaf, hardly controllable even with whip and goad. Now when the charioteer sees the vision of the loved one, so that a sensation of warmth spreads from him over the whole soul and he begins to feel an itching and the stings of desire, the obedient horse, constrained now as always by a sense of shame, holds himself back from springing upon the beloved; but the other, utterly heedless now of the driver's whip and goad, rushes forward prancing, and to the great discomfiture of his yoke-fellow and the charioteer drives them to approach the lad and make mention of the sweetness of physical love. At first the two indignantly resist the idea of being forced into such monstrous wrongdoing, but finally, when they can get no peace, they yield to the importunity of the bad horse and agree to do what he bids and advance. So they draw near, and the vision of the beloved dazzles their eyes. When the driver beholds it the sight awakens in him the memory of absolute beauty; he sees her again enthroned in her holy place attended by chastity. At the thought he falls upon his back in fear and awe, and in so doing inevitably tugs the reins so violently that he brings both horses down upon their haunches; the good horse gives way willingly and does not struggle, but the lustful horse resists with all his strength.

When they have withdrawn a little distance the good horse in shame and dread makes the whole soul break into a sweat, but the other no sooner recovers from the pain of the bit and of his fall than he bursts into angry abuse, reproaching the driver and his fellow horse for their cowardice and lack of spirit in running away and breaking their word. After one more attempt to force his unwilling partners to advance he grudgingly assents to their entreaty that the attempt should be deferred to another time. When that time comes they pretend to forget, but he reminds them; forcing them forward, neighing and tugging, he compels them to approach the beloved once more with the same suggestion. And when they come near he takes the bit between his teeth and pulls shamelessly, with head down and tail stretched out. The driver, however, experiences even more intensely what he experienced before; he falls back like a racing charioteer at the barrier, and with a still more violent backward pull jerks the bit from between the teeth of the lustful horse, drenches his abusive tongue and jaws with blood, and forcing his legs and haunches against the ground reduces him to torment. Finally, after several repetitions of this treatment, the wicked horse abandons his lustful ways; meekly now he executes the wishes of his driver, and when he catches sight of the loved one is ready to die of fear. So at last it comes about that the soul of the lover waits upon his beloved in reverence and awe.

Thus the beloved finds himself being treated like a god and receiving all manner of service from a lover whose love is true love and no pretence, and his own nature disposes him to feel kindly towards his admirer. He may repulse him at first because in the past he has imbibed from school-fellows and others the mistaken idea that is disgraceful to have dealings

42

with a lover, but as time goes on his increasing maturity and the decree of destiny bring him to admit his lover to his society; after all it is not ordained that bad men should be friends with one another, nor yet that good men should not. When he has made him welcome and begun to enjoy his conversation and society, the constant kindness that he meets with in close companionship with his lover strikes the beloved with amazement; he realizes clearly that all his other friends and relations together cannot offer him anything to compare with the affection that he receives from this friend whom a god has inspired. When their intimacy is established and the loved one has grown used to being near his friend and touching him in the gymnasium and elsewhere, the current of the stream which Zeus when he was in love with Ganymede called the 'stream of longing' sets in full flood towards the lover. Part of it enters into him, but when his heart is full the rest brims over, and as a wind or an echo rebounds from a smooth and solid surface and is carried back to its point of origin, so the stream of beauty returns once more to its source in the beauty of the beloved. It enters in at his eyes, the natural channel of communication with the soul, and reaching and arousing the soul moistens the passages from which the feathers shoot and stimulates the growth of wings, and in its turn the soul of the beloved is filled with love.

So now the beloved is in love, but with what he cannot tell. He does not know and cannot explain what has happened to him; he is like a man who has caught an eye infection from another and cannot account for it; he does not realize that he is seeing himself in his lover as in a glass. In his lover's presence he feels a relief from pain like his; when he is away he longs for him even as he himself is longed for. He is experiencing a counter-love which is the reflection of the love he inspires, but he speaks of it and thinks of it as friendship, not as love. Like his lover, though less strongly, he feels a desire to see, to touch, to kiss him, and to share his bed. And naturally it is not long before these desires are fulfilled in action. When they are in bed together, the lover's unruly horse has a word to say to his driver, and claims to be allowed a little enjoyment in return for all that he has suffered. But his counterpart in the beloved has nothing to say; but swelling with a desire of whose nature he is ignorant he embraces and kisses his lover as a demonstration of affection to so kind a friend, and when they are in each other's arms he is in a mood to refuse no favour that the lover may ask; yet his yoke-fellow in his turn joins with the charioteer in opposing to this impulse the moderating influence of modesty and reason. So, if the higher elements in their minds prevail, and guide them into a way of life which is strictly devoted to the pursuit of wisdom, they will pass their time on earth in happiness and harmony; by subduing the part of the soul that contained the seeds of vice and setting free that in which virtue had its birth they will become masters of themselves and their souls will be at peace. Finally, when this life is ended, their wings will carry them aloft; they will have won the first of the three bouts in the real Olympian Games, the greatest blessing that either human virtue or divine madness can confer on man.

But if they practise a less exalted way of life and devote themselves to the pursuit of honour rather than of wisdom, it may come about that in their cups or at some other unguarded moment their two unruly beasts will catch them unaware, and joining forces constrain them to snatch at what the world regards as the height of felicity and to consummate their

44

desire. Once they have enjoyed this pleasure they will enjoy it again thereafter, but sparingly, because what they do does not carry with it the consent of their whole mind. Though their friendship is upon a lower plane, such a pair too will remain friends, not only while their passion lasts but after it has abated; they will regard themselves as having exchanged mutual pledges so sacred that they can never without great guilt break them and become enemies. In the end they emerge from the body without wings, it is true, but having made a strong effort to achieve them; this is no mean prize, and it comes to them from the madness of love. Those who have already begun their heavenward journey the law does not compel to go down into the darkness beneath the earth: they pass their time journeying happily together in the brightness of day, and together, when the time comes, they receive their wings, because of their love.

Such, my son, are the divine blessings which will accrue to you from the friendship of a lover. But intimacy with one who is not in love, mangled as it is with worldly calculation and dispensing worldly advantages with a grudging hand, will breed in your soul the ignoble qualities which the multitude extols as virtues, and condemn you to wander for nine thousand years around and beneath the earth devoid of wisdom.

This speech, dear God of Love, I offer to thee in reparation as the best and finest palinode that my powers can devise. If its language in particular is perforce the language of poetry, the responsibility lies at Phaedrus' door. Grant me forgiveness for my former words and let these that I have now uttered find favour in thy sight. Deal kindly and graciously with me, and do not in anger take away or impair the skill in the science of love which thou hast given me; rather let me increase in honour in the sight of those that have beauty. If in the beginning Phaedrus and I uttered aught that offended thy ears, lay it to the account of Lysias, the true begetter of that speech, and make him cease from such words; turn his heart to the love of wisdom, even as the heart of Polemarchus his brother is turned, so that this his loving disciple may no longer be in two minds, as he is now, but may employ his life in philosophic discussion directed towards love in singleness of heart.

INTRODUCTION TO THE DISCUSSION OF RHETORIC.
THE MYTH OF THE CICADAS.

PHAEDRUS: I say Amen to that prayer, Socrates; so may it be if so it is best for us. All this time I have been lost in wonder at the immense superiority of this speech over that which preceded it; indeed, I am afraid that Lysias may appear feeble in comparison, supposing that he is prepared to match against it another speech of his own. But in fact, my dear Socrates, one of our politicians was recently making this very thing the subject of a diatribe against Lysias; the sum of all his reproaches was that Lysias is a writer of speeches. So it may be that regard for his reputation will keep him from writing any more.

SOCRATES: A preposterous notion, my dear young man. You are far astray in your judgement of your friend if you suppose him a man to be frightened by mere words. But perhaps you think that his critic really meant what he said to be a reproach?

PHAEDRUS: He certainly gave me that impression. And you yourself, Socrates, are perfectly well aware, I'm sure, that those who occupy the positions of greatest power and dignity in our states are ashamed to write speeches or to leave written compositions behind them, because they are afraid that posterity may give them the name of sophists.

SOCRATES: It's a case of Pleasant Bend, Phaedrus. You've forgotten that it is the *long* bend in the Nile which gives rise to that euphemism, and you've forgotten too that the politicians with the highest opinion of themselves are the most passionately anxious to write speeches and leave compositions behind them; why, whenever they write anything, they are so keen to win approval that they preface it with a clause containing the names of those who approve whatever that particular speech may contain.

PHAEDRUS: What do you mean? I don't follow you.

SOCRATES: Aren't you aware that any document composed by a politician is headed by the names of those who approve it?

PHAEDRUS: Explain yourself.

SOCRATES: 'Resolved', he begins, 'by the Council' or 'by the Assembly' or by both, and then goes on 'Moved by so-and-so', a splendidly pompous bit of self-advertisement on the part of the author. After that comes the body of his proposal, in which he displays his own wisdom to his supporters, sometimes in a composition of considerable length. Can you describe a document of this kind as anything but a speech committed to writing?

PHAEDRUS: No.

SOCRATES: Well, if he carries the day, the author leaves the stage triumphant, but if his motion is rejected and he loses his position as a recognized writer of speeches of this kind, he and his friends are plunged in gloom.

PHAEDRUS: They are indeed.

SOCRATES: Obviously their attitude to this occupation is one of admiration, not of contempt.

PHAEDRUS: Unquestionably.

SOCRATES: Again, when an orator or a king reaches a position of power like Lycurgus or Solon or Darius, and acquires immortality in his country as a writer of speeches, does he not in his own lifetime think himself the equal of the gods, and does not posterity agree in this estimate of him when it contemplates his productions?

PHAEDRUS: Certainly.

SOCRATES: Do you think then that any man of affairs, whoever he may be and however much an enemy of Lysias, seriously holds it against him that he is an author?

PHAEDRUS: Not if what you say is true, for in that case he would be criticizing his own darling pursuit.

SOCRATES: Then it must be clear to everybody that there is nothing inherently disgraceful in speech-writing.

PHAEDRUS: Agreed.

SOCRATES: The disgrace comes, I take it, when one speaks and writes disgracefully and badly instead of well.

PHAEDRUS: Obviously.

SOCRATES: How then are we to distinguish between good and bad writing? Shall we have to consult Lysias on the subject or anyone else who has written or is going to write? The nature of the writing does not signify; it may be on either public or private matters, either in verse or prose.

PHAEDRUS: Shall we have to consult, you ask. What would be the point of existing at all if it were not for pleasures such as these? Certainly life is not worth living for pleasures whose enjoyment entirely depends on a previous sensation of pain,

48

like almost all physical pleasures; that is why the latter are rightly called the pleasures of slaves.

SOCRATES: Well, we seem to have time at our disposal. What is more, I cannot help fancying that the cicadas overhead, singing and chattering to one another as their habit is in stifling heat, are watching us too. If they were to see us doing what most people do in the middle of the day, nodding under their soothing spell from sheer mental indolence instead of conversing, they would be entitled to laugh at us; they would take us for a pair of slaves that had invaded their haunt and were taking their midday nap near the spring, like sheep. But if they see us in conversation and realize that we are as deaf to their spells as if we were sailing past the Sirens, it may be that in admiration they will grant us the boon which heaven allows them to confer on mortal men.

PHAEDRUS: What boon is that? I don't think I have heard of it.

SOCRATES: It is most unfitting that a lover of the Muses should be ignorant of such a matter. The story is that once, before the birth of the Muses, cicadas were human beings. When the Muses were born and song came into the world, some of the men of that age were so ravished by its sweetness that in their devotion to singing they took no thought to eat and drink, and actually died before they knew what was happening to them. From them sprang thereafter the race of cicadas, to whom the Muses granted the privilege that they should need no food, but should sing from the moment of birth till death without eating and drinking, and after that go to the Muses and tell how each of them is honoured on earth and by whom. So the cicadas make report to Terpsichore of those who have honoured her in the dance, and thus win her favour for them;

to Erato of those who have occupied themselves in matters erotic, and similarly to the other Muses, according to the nature of the activity over which each Muse presides. But to Calliope the eldest of the Muses and her next sister Urania they make report of those who spend their lives in philosophy and honour the pursuit which owes its inspiration to these goddesses; among the Muses it is these that concern themselves with the heavens and the whole story of existence, divine and human, and their theme is the finest of them all. So you see that there are many reasons why we should proceed with our discussion instead of indulging in a midday sleep.

PHAEDRUS: Of course we must proceed with it.

SOCRATES: Then we must examine the question we propounded just now, what constitutes excellence and its opposite in speaking and writing.

PHAEDRUS: That is obvious.

THE NECESSITY OF KNOWLEDGE FOR A
TRUE ART OF RHETORIC

SOCRATES: Well, if a speech is to be classed as excellent, does not that presuppose knowledge of the truth about the subject of the speech in the mind of the speaker?

PHAEDRUS: But I have been told, my dear Socrates, that what a budding orator needs to know is not what is really right, but what is likely to seem right in the eyes of the mass of people who are going to pass judgement: not what is really good or fine but what will seem so; and that it is this rather than truth that produces conviction.

SOCRATES: 'Not to be lightly regarded', Phaedrus, is any word from the lips of the wise. On the contrary, we must see whether they may not be right, and in particular we must not dismiss what you have just said.

PHAEDRUS: Quite so.

SOCRATES: Let us look at it like this.

PHAEDRUS: How?

SOCRATES: Suppose I am trying to persuade you to buy a horse for service on a campaign. Neither of us knows exactly what a horse is, but I happen to know this much about you — Phaedrus believes a horse to be the longest-eared of the domestic animals.

PHAEDRUS: A ludicrous idea, Socrates.

SOCRATES: Wait a moment. Suppose that in a serious effort to persuade you I make use of a piece that I have composed in praise of the donkey. I call the donkey a horse, and tell you that the beast is highly serviceable both at home and in the field; you can use it to fight on, and to carry your baggage besides, and for many other purposes.

PHAEDRUS: That would be the height of absurdity.

SOCRATES: Isn't it better to be an absurd friend than a clever enemy?

PHAEDRUS: Of course.

SOCRATES: Well, when a speaker who does not know the difference between good and evil tries to convince a people as ignorant as himself, not by ascribing to a poor beast like a donkey the virtues of a horse, but by representing evil as in fact good, and so by a careful study of popular notions succeeds in persuading them to do evil instead of good, what kind of harvest do you think his rhetoric will reap from the seed he has sown?

PHAEDRUS: No very satisfactory harvest, I should say.

SOCRATES: But can it be, my friend, that we have treated the art of speech-making more roughly than we should? Perhaps she might reply: 'What nonsense is this, my good sirs? I do not insist on ignorance of truth as an essential qualification for the would-be speaker; for what my advice is worth I suggest that he should acquire that knowledge before embarking on me. I do emphatically assert, however, that without my assistance the man who knows the truth will make no progress in the art of persuasion.'

PHAEDRUS: If she says that, will she not be right?

SOCRATES: Yes, if the arguments that she still has to encounter support her claim to be an art. I think I hear some of them approaching and testifying that she is lying, and that she is not an art at all but a knack which has nothing to do with art. There is not nor ever shall be, as the Spartan said, a genuine art of speaking which is divorced from grasp of the truth.

PHAEDRUS: We need these arguments, Socrates. Bring them on and ask them what they mean.

SOCRATES: Come forward, noble creatures, and persuade Phaedrus, who begets such lovely children, that unless he becomes an adequate philosopher he will never be an adequate speaker either on any subject. And let Phaedrus answer.

PHAEDRUS: Ask your questions.

SOCRATES: Well, to give a general definition, is not the art of rhetoric a method of influencing men's minds by means of words, whether the words are spoken in a court of law or before some other public body or in private conversation? And is not the same art involved whatever the importance of the subject under discussion, so that it is no more creditable to use it correctly on a serious matter than on a trifle? Is that what you have been told of its nature?

PHAEDRUS: Oh no, not quite that. Lectures and writings on rhetoric as an art generally confine themselves to forensic oratory, though sometimes the former include political oratory as well. I have never heard the term used in a wider sense than that.

SOCRATES: Can it be that you have heard only of the treatises on the art of speaking composed by Nestor and Odysseus in their moments of leisure at Troy, and never of that of Palamedes?

PHAEDRUS: I have never heard even of that of Nestor, unless you are casting Gorgias for the part of Nestor, and Thrasymachus or Theodorus for that of Odysseus.

SOCRATES: Perhaps I am. But never mind them for the moment. Tell me, what is it that the opposing parties in a court of law engage in? Can we call it anything but a verbal contest?

PHAEDRUS: No, that is exactly what it is.

SOCRATES: About what is just and unjust?

PHAEDRUS: Yes.

SOCRATES: Then the man who follows the rules of the art will make the same jury think the same action just one moment and unjust the next, as he pleases?

PHAEDRUS: Of course.

SOCRATES: And in political speeches he will make his audience approve a course of action at one time and reject the same course at another?

PHAEDRUS: He will.

SOCRATES: But what about our Palamedes from Elea? Isn't it well known that he employs an art of speaking which makes his hearers think that the same objects are both like and unlike, both one and many, both at rest and in motion?

PHAEDRUS: True.

SOCRATES: Then the art of controversy is not confined to law or politics; every kind of discussion, it appears, is covered by one and the same art, if it is an art, and by means of it a man can make anything appear like anything else within the limits of possible comparison, and expose an opponent when he attempts to perform the same feat without being detected.

PHAEDRUS: What is all this leading to?

SOCRATES: We shall see, I think, if we ask the following question. Is a great or a slight difference between two things the more likely to be misleading?

PHAEDRUS: A slight difference.

SOCRATES: So if you proceed by small degrees from one thing to its opposite you are more likely to escape detection than if you take big steps.

PHAEDRUS: Of course.

SOCRATES: Then a man who sets out to mislead without being misled himself must have an exact knowledge of the likenesses and unlikenesses between things.

PHAEDRUS: That is essential.

SOCRATES: If he does not know the true nature of any given thing, how can he discover in other things a likeness to what he does not know, and decide whether the resemblance is small or great?

PHAEDRUS: He cannot.

SOCRATES: Now, when people's opinions are inconsistent with fact and they are misled, plainly it is certain resemblances that are responsible for mistakes creeping into their minds.

PHAEDRUS: Yes, that is how it happens.

SOCRATES: Is it possible then for a man to be skilled in leading the minds of his hearers by small gradations of difference in any given instance from truth to its opposite, or to escape being misled himself, unless he is acquainted with the true nature of the thing in question?

PHAEDRUS: Quite impossible.

SOCRATES: It seems then, my friend, that the art of speaking displayed by a man who has gone hunting after opinions instead of learning the truth will be a pretty ridiculous sort of art, in fact no art at all.

PHAEDRUS: It looks like it.

SOCRATES: Would you like us then to look at some examples of what we call genuine art and its opposite in the speech of Lysias which you are carrying and in the speeches which we delivered?

PHAEDRUS: There is nothing I should like better. At present we are arguing in the abstract for lack of suitable illustrations.

SOCRATES: Well, by a lucky accident the two speeches provide an example of how a speaker who knows the truth can make fun of his hearers and lead them astray. My own belief, Phaedrus, is that the local divinities are responsible for this; or it may be the interpreters of the Muses, the sweet singers overhead, that have been kind enough to inspire us, since for my part I lay no claim to any proficiency in the art of speaking.

PHAEDRUS: Put it down to them if you like; only please explain your meaning.

SOCRATES: Read me again the opening of Lysias' speech.

PHAEDRUS: 'You know my situation, and you have heard how I think that it will be to our advantage for this to happen. I beg you not to reject my suit because I am not in love with you. Lovers repent —'

SOCRATES: That will do. Now where does Lysias go wrong

and show absence of art? That is what we have to demon-strate, isn't it?

PHAEDRUS: Yes.

SOCRATES: Well, is it not perfectly obvious that there are some words about which we are in agreement, and others about which we differ?

PHAEDRUS: I think I see your meaning, but amplify it, please.

SOCRATES: When someone uses the words 'iron' or 'silver' we all have the same idea in our minds, haven't we?

PHAEDRUS: Certainly.

SOCRATES: But suppose the words used are 'just' or 'good'. Don't we then go each his own way, and find ourselves in disagreement with ourselves as well as with each other?

PHAEDRUS: Undoubtedly.

SOCRATES: So in some cases we are in agreement and in others not.

PHAEDRUS: Yes.

SOCRATES: In which case are we more liable to be misled, and in which is the art of speaking more effective?

PHAEDRUS: When the meaning of the word is uncertain, obviously.

SOCRATES: Then the man who embarks on the search for an art of speaking must first of all make a methodical classifi-cation, and find a distinguishing mark for each of the two kinds of words, those which in popular usage are bound to be ambiguous and those which are not.

PHAEDRUS: The man who grasps that will have made a very fine discovery, Socrates.

SOCRATES: Next, when he has to deal with a given subject, it must be perfectly clear to him, without any possibility of mis-take, to which class the subject of his speech belongs.

PHAEDRUS: Of course.

SOCRATES: What of love then? Is it to be classified as ambiguous or unambiguous?

PHAEDRUS: Ambiguous, obviously. Otherwise, how would it have been possible for you to describe it as you did just now as a curse to lover and loved alike, and then to turn round and assert that it is the greatest of blessings?

SOCRATES: An excellent point. But tell me – I've been so carried out of myself that I've quite forgotten – did I define love at the beginning of my speech?

PHAEDRUS: You did indeed, in the most emphatic manner conceivable.

SOCRATES: Dear me, by your account the nymphs of Achelous and Pan the son of Hermes are much greater experts in the art of speaking than Lysias the son of Cephalus. Or am I wrong, and did Lysias at the start of his encomium compel us to conceive of love as a definite thing on the meaning of which he had decided, and did he bring everything else in the whole course of his speech into conformity with that decision? Would you care to read his opening once more?

PHAEDRUS: As you please, but what you are looking for isn't there.

SOCRATES: Read it all the same, so that I can hear his own words.

PHAEDRUS: 'You know my situation, and you have heard how I think that it will be to our advantage for this to happen. I beg you not to reject my suit because I am not in love with you. Lovers repent the kindnesses they have shown when their passion abates.'

SOCRATES: You see how far Lysias is from doing what we are looking for. He is like a man swimming on his back, in reverse;

his speech begins where it should have ended, and his opening words are what the lover should say to his darling when his speech is finished. Or am I mistaken, my dear Phaedrus?

PHAEDRUS: I grant you that what he is talking of is what one would expect to find in a peroration, Socrates.

SOCRATES: Then again, don't the various parts of his speech give the impression of being thrown together at random? Do you see any intrinsic reason why the second topic, rather than any of the others, should be placed second? I am an ignoramus, of course, but it seemed to me that the writer showed a fine carelessness by saying whatever occurred to him. Can you point out any compelling rhetorical reason why he should have put his arguments together in the order he has?

PHAEDRUS: You do me too much honour if you suppose that I am capable of divining his motives so exactly.

SOCRATES: But I think you would agree that any speech ought to have its own organic shape, like a living being; it must not be without either head or feet; it must have a middle and extremities so composed as to fit one another and the work as a whole.

PHAEDRUS: Of course.

SOCRATES: Well, now look at your friend's speech and see whether it conforms to this criticism. You will find that it is no better than the epitaph said to have been inscribed on the tomb of Midas the Phrygian.

PHAEDRUS: What epitaph is that and what is the matter with it?

SOCRATES: It goes like this:

> A girl of bronze on Midas' tomb I stand,
> As long as water flows and trees grow tall,
> Remaining here on his lamented tomb,
> I'll tell to all who pass 'Here Midas lies'.

You notice, I am sure, that it is of no consequence what order these lines are spoken in.

PHAEDRUS: You are making fun of our speech, Socrates.

THE SPEECHES OF SOCRATES ILLUSTRATE A NEW PHILOSOPHICAL METHOD

SOCRATES: Well, I don't want to vex you, so we will let it pass, although it seems to me to contain a number of features which an observer would profit by not attempting to imitate. Let us turn to the other speeches; they contained something, I think, worth the attention of the student of rhetoric.

PHAEDRUS: What do you mean?

SOCRATES: They were, you remember, opposites; one maintained that a lover's desires should be gratified, and the other a non-lover's.

PHAEDRUS: And in both cases you argued like a man.

SOCRATES: I thought you were going to say like a madman, which would be no more than the truth. And that brings me to the very point I wished to make. We said that love was a kind of madness, didn't we?

PHAEDRUS: Yes.

SOCRATES: And that there are two types of madness, one arising from human disease, the other when heaven sets us free from established convention.

PHAEDRUS: Agreed.

SOCRATES: And we distinguished four kinds of divine madness and ascribed them to four divinities, the inspiration of the prophet to Apollo, that of the mystic to Dionysus, that of the poet to the Muses, and the fourth kind to

Aphrodite and Love; and of the four we declared the last, the madness of the lover, to be the best. And in trying to tell what the emotion of love is like it may be that we hit upon some truth, though in some respects perhaps we went astray. Anyhow, the mixture resulted in a not entirely unconvincing speech, a mythical hymn which celebrates in suitably devotional language the praises of Love, who is your master and mine, Phaedrus, and the protector of the young and fair.

PHAEDRUS: I certainly took great pleasure in hearing it.

SOCRATES: Let us then concentrate our attention on this single point, the way in which the transition from blame to praise was effected.

PHAEDRUS: What do you mean to deduce from that?

SOCRATES: My view is that, though the rest of the speech was really no more than a *jeu d'esprit*, yet in its random utterances two methods of reasoning can be discerned, and that it would be no bad thing if one could get a clear scientific idea of their function.

PHAEDRUS: What are these methods?

SOCRATES: The first method is to take a synoptic view of many scattered particulars and collect them under a single generic term, so as to form a definition in each case and make clear the exact nature of the subject one proposes to expound. So in our recent speech on love we began by defining what love is. That definition may have been good or bad, but at least it enabled the argument to proceed with clearness and consistency.

PHAEDRUS: What is the other method you have in mind, Socrates?

SOCRATES: The ability to divide a genus into species again,

observing the natural articulation, not mangling any of the parts, like an unskilful butcher. Take my two speeches just now. Both took irrationality as a generic notion. But just as in a single physical body there are pairs of organs with the same name but distinguished as left and right respectively, so in our two speeches: both postulated madness as a single generic form existing in us, but the first separated the left-hand part, as it were, and broke it down into further parts and did not give up till it detected among them what may be called a left-hand kind of love, which it very properly reprobated; whereas the second directed our attention to the types of madness on the right-hand side, and, finding there a kind of love which has the same name as the other but is divine, held it up before our eyes and eulogized it as the source of the greatest blessings that can fall to our lot.

PHAEDRUS: Perfectly true.

SOCRATES: Well, Phaedrus, I am a great lover of these methods of division and collection as instruments which enable me to speak and to think, and when I believe that I have found in anyone else the ability to discuss unity and plurality as they exist in the nature of things, I follow in his footsteps 'like the footsteps of god'. Hitherto I have given those who possess this ability the title of dialecticians, though heaven knows if I am right to do so. It is for you now to tell me what one ought to call them if one takes yourself and Lysias for one's masters. Can it be that what I have been describing is precisely that art of rhetoric to which Thrasymachus and the rest owe their ability not only to speak themselves but to make a good speaker of anyone who is prepared to pay them tribute as if they were kings?

PHAEDRUS: They may behave like kings, but they are quite

ignorant of the kind of knowledge you are asking about. You are quite right, I am sure, to give the name of dialectic to the method you have described, but I believe that the nature of rhetoric is still eluding us.

SOCRATES: How can that be? Is there anything worth having that can be systematically acquired if it is divorced from dialectic? If so, you and I should certainly not despise it. But what is rhetoric, what is left of it? That is the question that must be answered.

PHAEDRUS: There is a great deal left, Socrates, the whole contents, in fact, of the technical treatises on the subject.

A REVIEW OF THE DEVICES AND TECHNICAL TERMS OF CONTEMPORARY RHETORIC

SOCRATES: Thank you for reminding me. The first point, I suppose, is that a speech must begin with an 'introduction'. That is the sort of thing you mean, isn't it, the technical refinements of composition?

PHAEDRUS: Yes.

SOCRATES: Next must come a 'statement of the facts' supported by the evidence of witnesses; after that 'indirect evidence'; fourthly 'arguments from probability'; not to mention the 'proof' and 'supplementary proof' distinguished by that expert in rhetorical subtlety from Byzantium.

PHAEDRUS: Are you referring to the worthy Theodorus?

SOCRATES: Of course I am. And besides these one must include a 'refutation' and a 'subsidiary refutation', whether one is acting for the prosecution or the defence. And are we to leave out of account the admirable Evenus of Paros, the inventor of 'insinuation' and 'indirect compliments'? Some say that he also composed metrical examples of 'indirect blame', to serve as mnemonics – there was no end to the cleverness of the man. Then there are Tisias and Gorgias. Shall we leave buried in oblivion men who saw that probability is to be rated higher than truth, and who could make trivial matters appear great and great matters trivial simply by the forcefulness of their speech, besides discovering how to clothe new ideas in fine old language and to refurbish old thoughts by novel treatment, and to speak on any subject either compendiously or at infinite length? Once, however, when Prodicus heard me talking of this last accomplishment, he burst out laughing, and declared that he alone had found the secret of artistic oratory, which is that speeches should be neither long nor short but of suitable compass.

PHAEDRUS: Well done, Prodicus – what a brilliant discovery!

SOCRATES: And what of Hippias? The stranger from Elis would agree, I think, with Prodicus.

PHAEDRUS: Undoubtedly.

SOCRATES: Then there is Polus. What are we to say of his *Muses' Treasury of Speech*, with its 'Style Repetitive', its 'Style Sententious', and its 'Style Metaphorical', not to speak of the terms Licymnius presented him with as a contribution to his ornate style?

PHAEDRUS: But was there not something similar by Protagoras, Socrates?

SOCRATES: Yes, my lad, you mean his *Correct Diction*, and many other admirable works. But in the art of composing pathetic speeches bearing upon old age and poverty the master of them all in my opinion is the mighty man of Chalcedon.

He was expert also in rousing a crowd to fury, and then soothing its fury again by the spell of his words, to use his own expression; and in casting aspersions and removing them on any grounds or none he was unrivalled. To pass on, however. There seems to be general agreement about the ending of a speech; some call it recapitulation, while others give it different names.

PHAEDRUS: You mean refreshing the memory of the audience by giving at the end a brief summary of the various points in the speech?

SOCRATES: Exactly. Now is there anything else that you would like to add about the art of rhetoric?

PHAEDRUS: Only a few things hardly worth mentioning.

SOCRATES: Then never mind them. Let us rather hold what we have got up to the light, and examine what effect these technicalities produce and on what occasions.

PHAEDRUS: A very powerful effect, Socrates, at any rate in popular assemblies.

SOCRATES: No doubt. But look close, my good friend, and see whether the texture of the stuff seems as threadbare to you as it does to me.

PHAEDRUS: I should like you to demonstrate it.

SOCRATES: Very well. Now, if someone came to your friend Eryximachus or his father Acumenus and said that by the application of certain substances to the body of a patient he could induce at will heat or cold, or, if he thought fit, vomiting or purging, and so on, and by virtue of this knowledge claimed to be a doctor or to be able to make a doctor of anyone to whom he imparted it, what do you think his hearers would say?

PHAEDRUS: Obviously they would ask whether he also knew

what patients should be subjected to each of these treatments, and when, and to what extent.

SOCRATES: Suppose he were to answer: 'Of course not. I expect my pupil to be able to find out what you ask for himself.'

PHAEDRUS: Then no doubt they would say: 'This man is mad. He has read something in a book or lit upon certain prescriptions by chance, and believes himself to be a doctor when he knows nothing of the art of medicine.'

SOCRATES: Or suppose a man were to approach Sophocles and Euripides and say that he knew how to compose lengthy speeches about trifles and very concise ones about matters of importance, and that he could turn out at will passages of deep pathos or at the other extreme tirades full of fury and menace, or produce any other effect to order, and claimed that by imparting these skills he could in fact deliver the recipe for a tragedy?

PHAEDRUS: As in the other instance, Socrates, his hearers would doubtless laugh at a man who did not realize that what makes a tragedy is the combination of these elements in such a way as to harmonize with each other and with the whole.

SOCRATES: But instead of indulging in vulgar abuse they would, I am sure, be more likely to behave like a musician when he encounters someone who, because he knows how to strike the highest and lowest possible notes, believes that he is a master of harmony. The musician will not say roughly: 'My poor man, you're daft.' On the contrary, being a musician he will use gentler language and say: 'It is quite true, my good sir, that anyone who aspires to master harmony must possess the knowledge you have acquired, but a man in your position may for all that be quite ignorant of harmony. What you have is not knowledge of harmony but only an indispensable preliminary to such knowledge.'

PHAEDRUS: Absolutely right.

SOCRATES: So Sophocles would tell the man who was showing off to him and Euripides that his ability was merely a necessary preliminary to the tragic art, not the art itself, and Acumenus would make a similar answer about medicine.

PHAEDRUS: Of course they would.

SOCRATES: Well then. Suppose that honey-tongued Adrastus or even Pericles were to hear talk of these fine devices of concise expression and metaphorical expression and the like, which we said must be gone through and held up to the light to be examined. Do you think they would imitate the vulgar behaviour of people like you and me, and content themselves with hurling a rough and uncultivated phrase at those who have taught and written about these devices as the whole art of rhetoric? Would they not rather, out of their superior wisdom, find fault with us and say: 'Instead of losing your temper, Phaedrus and Socrates, you should make allowances for those who, because they do not understand dialectical method, have proved unable to define the nature of rhetoric, and have believed in consequence that they have discovered the art itself, when all that they have got hold of is the knowledge which is a necessary preliminary to it.' They think that by imparting this knowledge they have perfectly discharged the task of a teacher of rhetoric, and that the use of each of these devices so as to produce conviction and the composition of a consistent whole is a simple matter which their pupils must work out for themselves when they come to make speeches.

PHAEDRUS: I believe you are right, Socrates. It looks as if the art which such people teach and write about as the art of rhetoric is no more than you say. But in that case how and where is one to acquire the genuine art of the convincing speaker?

RHETORIC AND PHILOSOPHY

SOCRATES: If you mean the power to become a finished performer, Phaedrus, it seems likely – indeed, inevitable – that what is true of everything else holds good here also. If you have a natural gift for speaking you will become a famous speaker, provided that you improve your gift by knowledge and practice, but if any of these conditions is unfulfilled you will to that extent fall short of your goal. In so far as it is a matter of art the method which appeals to me is not the method which is pursued by Lysias and Thrasymachus.

PHAEDRUS: What is it then?

SOCRATES: I fancy, my friend, that it was not surprising that Pericles became the most finished speaker who has ever lived.

PHAEDRUS: Why do you say that?

SOCRATES: All the great arts need to be supplemented by philosophical chatter and daring speculation about the nature of things: from this source appear to come the sublimity of thought and all-round completeness which characterize them. Now Pericles added these qualities to his own natural gifts; he fell in with Anaxagoras, who was a thinker of this type, and by steeping himself in speculation arrived at a knowledge of the nature of reason and unreason, the favourite subject, no doubt, for Anaxagoras' discourse, from which Pericles drew and applied to the art of speaking whatever was relevant to it.

PHAEDRUS: How do you mean?

SOCRATES: The same is presumably true of the art of rhetoric as of the art of medicine.

PHAEDRUS: In what way?

SOCRATES: In both cases a nature needs to be analysed, in one the nature of the human body and in the other the nature of the soul. Without this any attempt to implant health and strength in the body by the use of drugs or diet, or the kind of conviction and excellence you desire in the soul by means of speeches and rules of behaviour, will be a matter of mere empirical knack and not of science.

PHAEDRUS: You may well be right, Socrates.

SOCRATES: How do you think it possible to form an adequate conception of the nature of an individual soul without considering the nature of soul in general?

PHAEDRUS: If we are to believe the Asclepiad doctor Hippocrates this method is equally essential in dealing with an individual body.

SOCRATES: Hippocrates is quite right, my friend. But Hippocrates' authority is not enough; we must see whether sound reason is on his side.

PHAEDRUS: Of course.

SOCRATES: What then have Hippocrates and Truth to say on this subject? Surely that if we are to form a clear notion of the nature of anything at all, we must first determine whether the subject on which we wish to acquire scientific knowledge ourselves and the ability to impart that knowledge to others is simple or complex. Next, if it is simple we must examine its natural function, both active and passive; what does it act upon and what acts upon it? If it is complex we must determine the number of its parts, and in the case of each of these go through the same process as applies to the simple whole; how and on what does it produce an effect, and how and by what is an effect produced upon it?

PHAEDRUS: It may be as you say, Socrates.

SOCRATES: Any other procedure would be like the groping of a blind man. We must not expose the scientific investigator of any subject to a comparison with the blind – or with the deaf, for that matter. Now, plainly, if one is to teach the art of speaking on scientific lines, one must demonstrate precisely the essential nature of the object to which the art is to be applied, and that object, I presume, is soul.

PHAEDRUS: Of course.

SOCRATES: Then it is towards soul that all the rhetorician's energy will be directed. It is there he aims to produce conviction, is it not?

PHAEDRUS: Yes.

SOCRATES: So it is clear that Thrasymachus and any other serious and scientific teacher of the art of speaking will regard it as his first duty to make us see as precisely as possible whether soul is naturally a homogeneous unity or complex, like body; that is what we mean by demonstrating its nature.

PHAEDRUS: Certainly.

SOCRATES: In the next place he will describe how and upon what it naturally acts, and how and by what it is acted upon, and to what effect.

PHAEDRUS: No doubt.

SOCRATES: Thirdly, he will classify the various types of speech and of soul, and the ways in which souls can be affected, and arrange them in corresponding pairs, giving reasons for his choice and showing why a particular sort of speech inevitably produces conviction in a particular sort of soul, and fails to do so in another.

PHAEDRUS: That would be the best way, it seems.

SOCRATES: Not merely the best but the only way, my dear Phaedrus; no other method of demonstration in speech or writing can be called scientific, whatever the subject it deals with. The existing writers of rhetorical manuals, whose lectures you have heard, are rogues: they are perfectly well aware of the truth about soul but choose to keep it from us. So we must not admit their claim to be scientific until they speak and write in the way I describe.

PHAEDRUS: What way do you mean?

SOCRATES: To give the actual words would be too much of a business, but I don't mind telling you how one ought to write if one wants to be as scientific as possible.

PHAEDRUS: Please do.

SOCRATES: The function of speech is to influence the soul. It follows that the would-be speaker must know how many types of soul there are. The number is finite, and they account for the variety of individual characters. When these have been determined one must enumerate the various types of speech, a finite number also. For such and such a reason a certain type of person can be easily persuaded to adopt a certain course of action by a certain type of speech, whereas for an equally valid reason a different type cannot. When the student has an adequate theoretical knowledge of these types, the next requisite is that his powers of observation should be keen enough to follow them up when he comes across them in actual life; otherwise he will be no better off for all the instruction received in the lecture room. When he is not only qualified to say what type of man is influenced by what type of speech, but is able also to single out a particular individual and make clear to himself that there he has actually before him a specific example of a type of character which he has heard described, and that this is what he must say and this is how he must say it if he wants to influence his hearer in this particular way — when, I say, he has grasped all this, and knows besides when to speak and when to refrain, and can distinguish when to employ and when to eschew the various rhetorical devices of conciseness and pathos and exaggeration and so on that he has learnt, then and not till then can he be said to have perfectly mastered his art. If his teaching or writing falls short in any of these respects we are entitled to reject his claim to be a properly qualified speaker. 'So,' our writer on this subject may say to us, 'here is my account of the art of speaking, Phaedrus and Socrates; are you satisfied with it, or do you want something different?'

PHAEDRUS: One cannot ask for anything different, Socrates. Nevertheless what is set before us is no small task.

SOCRATES: You are quite right. Before we undertake it we should make a thorough review of all we have said on the subject, in case there should be a quicker and easier way to our goal. A long, rough, roundabout route would be a waste of time if there is a short and smooth one. So if what you have heard from Lysias or anyone else can help us at all here, do your best to recollect it.

PHAEDRUS: It's not for want of trying, but I have nothing to offer at the moment.

SOCRATES: Would you like me then to give you an account of the matter which I heard from some who concern themselves with it?

PHAEDRUS: Of course.

SOCRATES: We are told, you know, Phaedrus, that it is legitimate to play the devil's advocate.

PHAEDRUS: Then please do so.

SOCRATES: Well, to their way of thinking there is no need to be so portentous or long-winded, or to make such uphill work of the matter. The fact is, as we said at the beginning of our discussion, that the aspiring speaker needs no knowledge of the truth about what is right or good, or about men whose nature or breeding has made them so. In courts of justice no attention whatever is paid to the truth about such topics; all that matters is plausibility. Plausibility is simply another name for probability, and probability is the thing to concentrate on if you would be a scientific speaker. There are even some occasions when both prosecution and defence should positively suppress the facts in favour of probability, if the facts are improbable. Never mind the truth – pursue probability through thick and thin in every kind of speech; the whole secret of the art of speaking lies in consistent adherence to this principle.

PHAEDRUS: This is what those who claim to be professional teachers of rhetoric actually say, Socrates. We touched briefly on this point at an earlier stage, I remember, and those who make this their concern attach crucial importance to it.

SOCRATES: Well, take Tisias; you've no doubt studied his book carefully. Let us ask Tisias then whether he means by probable anything more than what the public finds acceptable.

PHAEDRUS: What more could he mean?

SOCRATES: So it was as a result of this profound discovery about his art that Tisias wrote that if a brave pygmy is prosecuted for assaulting a cowardly giant and robbing him of his clothes neither of them should reveal the truth. The coward must declare that he was attacked by more than one man, whereas his opponent must maintain that no one else was present and fall back on the well-known line: 'How could a little chap like me have set upon a colossus like him?' The other of course will not admit his own poor spirit, but will produce some further lie which may provide his adversary with a chance of tripping him. And in other cases too these are the sort of 'scientific' rules that are enunciated. Isn't it so, Phaedrus?

PHAEDRUS: Unquestionably.

SOCRATES: Dear me, what a strangely recondite art we owe to the invention of Tisias or whoever it was and whatever he was pleased to take his name from. But, my dear Phaedrus, shall we or shall we not say to him –

PHAEDRUS: What?

SOCRATES: 'Tisias, for some time before you ever came on the scene we were saying that what you call probability establishes itself in the minds of the populace because of its likeness to truth; and we concluded that in every case such likenesses are best discovered by the man who knows the truth. So if you have anything further to say about the art of speaking we shall be glad to hear it; otherwise we shall accept the conclusion we have already reached that a man who does not distinguish the various natures among his audience, and who cannot analyse things into their species and classify individuals under a single form will never attain such mastery of the art of speaking as is open to man. This, however, is a goal that cannot be reached without great pains, which the wise man will undergo not with the object of addressing and dealing with human beings but in order to be able to the best of his power to say and do what is acceptable in the sight of heaven. Those who are wiser than we, Tisias, tell us that the object of a man of sense will not be the gratification of fellow-slaves, except incidentally, but of masters who are supremely good. It is no wonder then that the road is long and winding; the end to which it leads is a great end, different from the end which you propose to yourself; yet that, too, as our discussion shows, will best be reached, if a man has a mind to it, as a result of the other.'

PHAEDRUS: A magnificent theory, Socrates, I agree, if one could put it into practice.

SOCRATES: It is noble to aim at a noble goal, whatever the outcome.

PHAEDRUS: It is indeed.

SOCRATES: So much then for the genuine art of speaking and its opposite.

PHAEDRUS: Agreed.

THE INFERIORITY OF THE WRITTEN TO THE SPOKEN WORD

SOCRATES: There remains the question of the propriety and impropriety of writing, and the conditions which determine them. We have still to discuss that, haven't we?

PHAEDRUS: Yes.

SOCRATES: Do you know the theory and practice which will best please God, as far as words are concerned?

PHAEDRUS: No, I do not. Do you?

SOCRATES: Well, I can give you a tradition handed down from men of old, but they alone know the truth. If we could find that out for ourselves, should we have any further use for human fancies?

PHAEDRUS: An absurd question. But tell me your tradition.

SOCRATES: They say that there dwelt at Naucratis in Egypt one of the old gods of that country, to whom the bird they call Ibis was sacred, and the name of the god himself was Theuth. Among his inventions were number and calculation and geometry and astronomy, not to speak of various kinds of draughts and dice, and, above all, writing. The king of the whole country at that time was Thamus, who lived in the great city of Upper Egypt which the Greeks call Egyptian Thebes; the name they give to Thamus is Ammon. To him came Theuth and exhibited his inventions, claiming that they ought to be made known to the Egyptians in general. Thamus inquired into the use of each of them, and as Theuth went through them expressed approval or disapproval, according as he judged Theuth's claims to be well or ill founded. It would take too long to go through all that Thamus is reported to have said for and against each of Theuth's inventions. But when it came to writing, Theuth declared: 'Here is an accomplishment, my lord the king, which will improve both the wisdom and the memory of the Egyptians. I have discovered a sure receipt for memory and wisdom.' 'Theuth, my paragon of inventors,' replied the king, 'the discoverer of an art is not the best judge of the good or harm which will accrue to those who practise it. So it is in this case; you, who are the father of writing, have out of fondness for your offspring attributed to it quite the opposite of its real function. Those who acquire it will cease to exercise their memory and become forgetful; they will rely on writing to bring things to their remembrance by external signs instead of on their own internal resources.

75

What you have discovered is a receipt for recollection, not for memory. And as for wisdom, your pupils will have the reputation for it without the reality: they will receive a quantity of information without proper instruction, and in consequence be thought very knowledgeable when they are for the most part quite ignorant. And because they are filled with the conceit of wisdom instead of real wisdom they will be a burden to society.'

PHAEDRUS: How easy you find it, Socrates, to compose a story from Egypt or any other country.

SOCRATES: Well, Phaedrus, the priests in the sanctuary of Zeus at Dodona declared that the earliest oracles came from an oak tree, and the men of their time, who lacked your modern sophistication, were simple-minded enough to be quite satisfied with messages from an oak or a rock if only they were true. But truth is not enough for you; you think it matters who the speaker is and where he comes from.

PHAEDRUS: I accept the rebuke. What your Theban says about writing is quite sound, I'm sure.

SOCRATES: Then it shows great folly — as well as ignorance of the pronouncement of Ammon — to suppose that one can transmit or acquire clear and certain knowledge of an art through the medium of writing, or that written words can do more than remind the reader of what he already knows on any given subject.

PHAEDRUS: Quite right.

SOCRATES: The fact is, Phaedrus, that writing involves a similar disadvantage to painting. The productions of painting look like living beings, but if you ask them a question they maintain a solemn silence. The same holds true of written words; you might suppose that they understand what they are saying, but if you ask them what they mean by anything they simply return the same answer over and over again. Besides, once a thing is committed to writing it circulates equally among those who understand the subject and those who have no business with it; a writing cannot distinguish between suitable and unsuitable readers. And if it is ill-treated or unfairly abused it always needs its parent to come to its rescue; it is quite incapable of defending or helping itself.

PHAEDRUS: All that you say is absolutely just.

SOCRATES: Now can we distinguish another kind of communication which is the legitimate brother of written speech, and see how it comes into being and how much better and more effective it is?

PHAEDRUS: What kind do you mean and how does it come about?

SOCRATES: I mean the kind that is written on the soul of the hearer together with understanding; that knows how to defend itself, and can distinguish between those it should address and those in whose presence it should be silent.

PHAEDRUS: You mean the living and animate speech of a man with knowledge, of which written speech might fairly be called a kind of shadow.

SOCRATES: Exactly. Now tell me this. Would a sensible farmer take seed which he valued and wished to produce a crop, and sow it in sober earnest in gardens of Adonis at midsummer, and take pleasure in seeing it reach its full perfection in eight days? Isn't this something that he might do in a holiday mood by way of diversion, if he did it at all? But where he is serious he will follow the true principles of agriculture and sow his seed in soil that suits it, and be well satisfied if what he has sown comes to maturity eight months later.

PHAEDRUS: You do well to distinguish, Socrates, between the farmer's serious business and what he might do in a different spirit.

SOCRATES: And are we to say that the man with real knowledge of right and beauty and good will treat what we may by analogy call his seed less intelligently than the farmer?

PHAEDRUS: Of course not.

SOCRATES: Then when he is in earnest he will not take a pen and write in water or sow his seed in the black fluid called ink, to produce discourses which cannot defend themselves viva voce or give any adequate account of the truth.

PHAEDRUS: Presumably not.

SOCRATES: No, indeed. It will simply be by way of pastime that he will use the medium of writing to sow what may be styled gardens of literature, laying up for himself as well as for those who follow the same track aids to recollection against the time when the forgetfulness of old age may overtake him, and it will give him pleasure to see the growth of their tender shoots. And when other men resort to other diversions, and indulge themselves with drinking-parties and kindred pleasures, he on the contrary will amuse himself, I think, with the sort of pastime that I am describing.

PHAEDRUS: And a very fine pastime too, Socrates — as fine as the other is worthless. I mean the ability to amuse oneself with the composition of discourses about justice and the other subjects you mention.

SOCRATES: Quite so, my dear Phaedrus. But finer still is the serious treatment of these subjects which you find when a man employs the art of dialectic, and, fastening upon a suitable soul, plants and sows in it truths accompanied by knowledge. Such truths can defend themselves as well as the man who planted them; they are not sterile, but contain a seed from which fresh truths spring up in other minds; in this way they secure immortality for it, and confer upon the man who possesses it the highest happiness which it is possible for a human being to enjoy.

PHAEDRUS: The process you speak of is even more excellent.

SOCRATES: Then since that is agreed, Phaedrus, we can now consider our original problem.

RECAPITULATION AND CONCLUSION

PHAEDRUS: What problem do you mean?

SOCRATES: The problem which has led us to the present point in the search of its solution. We set out, if you remember, to examine the reproach incurred by Lysias by reason of his speech-writing, and to determine what constitutes science and lack of science in speech-writing as a whole. The second point we have, I think, satisfactorily cleared up.

PHAEDRUS: So it appeared. But remind me once more how it was done.

SOCRATES: Our whole previous discussion has proved that speeches, whether their aim is to instruct or to persuade, cannot be scientifically constructed, in so far as their nature allows of scientific treatment at all, unless the following conditions are fulfilled. In the first place a man must know the truth about any subject that he deals with, either in speech or writing; he must be able to define it generically, and having defined it to divide it into its various specific kinds until he reaches the limit of divisibility. Next, he must analyse on the same principles the nature of soul, and discover what type of speech is suitable for each type of soul. Finally, he must arrange and organize his speech accordingly, addressing a simple speech to a simple soul, but to those which are more complex something of greater complexity which embraces the whole range of tones.

PHAEDRUS: There can be no doubt that that was the conclusion we reached.

SOCRATES: Then to return to the original point, whether the composition and delivery of speeches is honourable or dishonourable, and in what circumstances it may fairly be reckoned a reproach or the reverse. Has not our previous discussion plainly shown –

PHAEDRUS: What has it shown?

SOCRATES: That Lysias or any other writer, past or future, who claims that clear and permanently valid truth is to be found in a written speech, lays himself open to reproach, whether that reproach is actually levelled at him or not. It makes no difference whether the speech is to be delivered in a private capacity or in support of a constitutional proposal, when it becomes in effect a political treatise. To be unable to distinguish between dream and waking reality about right and wrong, good and evil, is a condition which cannot escape censure, even though the populace as a whole may be loud in its praise.

PHAEDRUS: Certainly it cannot.

SOCRATES: To believe, on the other hand, that a written composition on any subject must be to a large extent the creation of fancy; that nothing worth serious attention has ever been written in prose or verse – or spoken for that matter, if by speaking one means the kind of recitation that aims merely at creating belief, without any attempt at instruction by question and answer; that even the best of such compositions can do no more than help the memory of those who already know; whereas lucidity and finality and serious importance are to be found only in words spoken by way of instruction or, to use a truer phrase, written on the soul of the hearer to enable him to learn about the right, the beautiful and the good; finally, to realize that such spoken truths are to be reckoned a man's legitimate sons, primarily if they originate within himself, but to a secondary degree if what we may call their children and kindred come to birth, as they should, in the minds of others – to believe this, I say, and to let all else go is to be the sort of man, Phaedrus, that you and I might well pray that we may both become.

PHAEDRUS: What you say expresses exactly my own wish and prayer.

SOCRATES: Then I think we may be content with the literary discussion with which we have been amusing ourselves. Go and tell Lysias that we two went down to the stream and shrine of the Nymphs and there received the following message which we are charged to deliver to Lysias and other speech-writers, to Homer and other poets, whether they compose for accompaniment or not, and finally to Solon and anyone who has written treatises in the form of political utterances, which he calls laws. If any of them had knowledge of the truth when he wrote, and can defend what he has written by submitting to an interrogation on the subject, and make it evident as soon as he speaks how comparatively inferior are his writings, such a one should take his title not from what he has written but from what has been the object of his serious pursuit.

PHAEDRUS: What is the title you have in mind for him?

SOCRATES: To call him wise, Phaedrus, would, I think, be excessive; God alone deserves to be so described. But to call him a lover of wisdom or something of the sort would be more appropriate and at the same time more modest.

PHAEDRUS: There would be nothing amiss in that.

SOCRATES: Then the man whose most precious production is what he has composed or written, and who has devoted his time to twisting words this way and that, pasting them together and pulling them apart, may fairly be called a poet or a speech-writer or a maker of laws.

PHAEDRUS: Of course.

SOCRATES: That then is the message you must take to your friend.

PHAEDRUS: But what about you? You have a friend too, and it would be just as wrong to neglect him.

SOCRATES: Whom do you mean?

PHAEDRUS: The fair Isocrates. What message will you take to him, Socrates, and how shall we describe him?

SOCRATES: Isocrates is still young, Phaedrus. But I don't mind telling you the future I foresee for him.

PHAEDRUS: Please do.

SOCRATES: He seems to me to have natural gifts superior to anything displayed in the speeches of Lysias, and the elements in his character make a nobler combination. So I should not be at all surprised if, as he grows older, he makes all his predecessors in the kind of composition in which he is now engaged look like children, or if he becomes dissatisfied with his present pursuits and is driven on by some divine inspiration to greater things. Nature, my dear Phaedrus, has not left the man devoid of a certain love of wisdom. That is the message that I am taking from the divinities here to Isocrates, who is my favourite, and you must take the other to Lysias, who is yours.

PHAEDRUS: Very well. Let us be going then, since the heat has abated.

SOCRATES: Surely we should first make a prayer to the powers of this place.

PHAEDRUS: Of course.

SOCRATES: 'Dear Pan and ye other gods who inhabit here, grant that I may become fair within, and that my external circumstances may be such as to further my inward health. May I esteem the wise man rich, and allow me no more wealth than a man of moderation can bear and manage.' Is there anything else that we should ask for, Phaedrus? To me my prayer seems sufficient.

PHAEDRUS: Offer it for me too, Socrates; friends should share everything.

SOCRATES: Let us be going.